Careers
in the
Theatre

Careers in the Theatre

Jean Richardson

Kogan
Page

Acknowledgements

The author would like to thank the following for their help: Kevin Cahill, education officer of the National Theatre; the press office of the RSC; the Greenwich Young People's Theatre; the National Youth Theatre; the drama schools and universities who sent prospectuses; the Job Centre Library, Farringdon Road; the National Council for Drama Training; The British Theatre Institute; the training officer of the Arts Council; Anthony John, Regional Theatre Trainee Director Scheme; Jonathan Brill of the Council for National Academic Awards; and Peter Finch, press and publicity officer of Equity.

First published 1983 by Kogan Page Limited
120 Pentonville Road, London N1 9JN

Copyright © Kogan Page 1983

British Library Cataloguing in Publication Data

Richardson, Jean
  Careers in the theatre.—(Kogan Page Careers series)
  1. Theatre — Vocational guidance — Great Britain
  I. Title
  792'.02'9341   PN2055

  ISBN 0-85038-641-1 (Hb)
  ISBN 0-85038-642-X (Pb)

Printed in Great Britain by
Spottiswoode and Ballantyne,
Colchester and London

Contents

Part 2

Part 1

Chapter 1
Up-Front

Introduction

'There's no business like show business' sings the chorus in *Annie Get Your Gun*, introducing what has since become one of the theme songs of the entertainments industry.

And, of course, there are no people like show people either; they 'smile when they are down' and wouldn't change the life for 'a sack of gold' because although one moment they may be down and out in the cold, 'next day on your dressing room they hang a star', which makes it all worth while.

The cruel divide between failure and success is a recurrent experience of life in the theatre. Like everything to do with the arts it is very demanding, and in return it gives uncertain, capricious rewards that bear little relation to the amount of work that has gone into an enterprise. The company can work like slaves and act like angels and then for some reason — fashions in taste, indifferent reviews — the public doesn't come and that's it. Even in highly subsidised companies, the theatre is ultimately about selling tickets and balancing the books.

The most obvious job in the theatre is up-front, on stage, behind the footlights, and when people think of working in the theatre they usually have in mind quite literally being on the stage. But the theatre involves a variety of other jobs, from directing, painting scenery, looking after costumes, being part of the stage crew, to working in the box office, designing programmes, dealing with the press;

and drama, a word often used for theatre as a study subject, can lead to a wide range of jobs outside the theatre: in education, in the media, in arts administration, as a drama therapist working in hospitals, prisons, or with the handicapped, in community work, and in industry, where role-playing is now used in management training.

Drama training itself can be vocational, ie designed to equip students for specific careers in the professional theatre, films and television, or non-vocational, as in the many degree and diploma courses that give students the chance to discover and develop their interests and are especially suitable for those who love the theatre but have neither the talent nor the ambition to go on the stage. This book includes pointers in a number of directions, but deals in detail only with careers within the theatre, both on stage and behind the scenes.

And since actors (and the word is intended to include both sexes) are the up-front people of the theatre, it seems appropriate to start with them, though much to be said applies also to other members of the theatre, who share the same discomforts and drawbacks.

Acting

Despite its superficial glamour, the stage is a heart-breaking, overcrowded profession. Unemployment is high: the actors' trade union Equity reckons that about 75 per cent of its members are out of work at any one time. Hours are long and unsocial: actors may spend most of the day rehearsing and then have to appear in an evening performance. It's hard on family life: as well as being out every night if they're working, theatre people have to be away from home on tour, where they are exposed to the delights of theatrical digs. The money isn't wonderful: although top actors and actresses do command large fees (usually from screen not stage appearances), many young actors and theatre staff don't earn more than £100 a week (and less outside London), and of course they are often out of work for some of the time. There's no security: although the National

Theatre, the Royal Shakespeare Company, the Chichester Festival Theatre and some regional theatres do engage actors for a season (the RSC is particularly generous in this respect), runs in the commercial theatre are notoriously unpredictable. There is only one *Mousetrap* (now in its thirty-first year), but a sorry number of productions that fail to make it to the West End or close after only a few weeks.

Actors

So what sort of people are actors and what makes them choose such an unpredictable career?

Their reasons are complex and perhaps to some extent unconscious. First, obviously, actors derive great satisfaction from the actual business of acting, from what is, at its simplest, dressing up and pretending to be someone else. It may seem a strange thing to enjoy so much, especially as the enjoyment is in a sense a need. In an interview, Sir Alec Guinness gave as his explanation: '. . . I think the springs lie either in the unhappiness and loneliness of childhood, making up stories for yourself and acting them out for yourself, or — for some people — in very happy childhoods of playing together.' Guinness also says that the relationship between acting and children's games suggests a certain childishness in the actor, an inability to grow up, whereas the writer Ronald Hayman, in his stimulating account of the theatre today, *The Set-Up*, sees the actor as having something in common with the schizophrenic, who is looking for an unreal, outer self behind which to hide.

While such ideas may seem to have little to do with a conscious decision to become an actor, the theatre undoubtedly appeals strongly to a certain kind of exhibitionist temperament, and actors are largely born not made. Peter Barkworth defines acting talent as 'a desire to get up and show off in front of people', while fellow actor Clive Swift comes to the uncompromising conclusion: 'Those who survive are those who need to act.'

So one thing any intending actor needs is a desire to act

rather than do anything else in the world. Then, of course, there is also talent.

Social background is and always has been unimportant, though it may be a help initially to have relations in the theatre; acting, like other talents, does seem to run in families — for example, the Redgraves — and as with other jobs there is a tendency to follow in father's, or mother's, footsteps. A certain kind of accent and looks are no longer the advantage they once were, because fashions in realism and working-class drama have brought a demand for ordinary looks and everyday speech, and there is now a shortage of convincing lords and ladies, not to say princes and princesses. There has also been a move away from the charismatic importance of the star to being a member of a company, but as the public will probably always have a weakness for charm and good looks, the handsome and the beautiful need not despair.

Like other freelance jobs acting appeals to the kind of person who likes to flirt with insecurity, though not all actors would endorse Sir Michael Hordern's positive relish for it: 'I also like the uncertainty of my profession. I want to wonder what's going to happen next, and to look forward to x months' time, when I know I'm going to be on the market again. I want to listen for that telephone call.' Such a temperament finds uncertainty adds a spice to life, is optimistic, and has the ability to take life as it comes and feel that something good is about to turn up — which for such a person it often does. But this is not to say that most actors aren't worried sick when they're out of work . . .

Actors also need to be physically and mentally tough. Acting is a draining experience that generates the kind of excitement — a feeling of being high — that can overcome tiredness during a performance. Apart from exhausting rehearsals — which sometimes have to be coupled with an evening performance — many parts are physically tiring, calling for actors to memorise complicated moves, wear uncomfortable and often heavy clothes and make-up, perform dangerous feats such as duelling or flying, as well as having to cope with an audience which may be disappointingly small, unresponsive, or even hostile. During rehearsals an actor may also have to cope with criticism and sarcasm from a demanding, dissatisfied director who has the power to get rid of him or her, or see that the contract is not renewed. No one should take up acting without being aware of such pressures, which can be masked by the glamour of the actor on stage.

Perhaps because of their basic insecurity, actors tend to present an outward image of gregariousness and loyalty — any awards ceremony is always an occasion for affectionate backslapping and indiscriminate praise. Relationships are forged on tour, in theatrical digs, in long runs, and it's a relatively small world, with the same faces meeting up again and tipping off each other about work. There is a certain ambivalence between getting oneself work and helping friends, and it's impossible to categorise the ways in which actors and backstage staff hear about and get work.

Although in the past actors often had little formal training but would join a company in some humble capacity, make the tea, walk on carrying a spear and learn by a mixture of example and trial and error, the actor of today needs proper training at a drama school.

But the theatre has become a many-headed hydra with tentacles that reach out into many spheres, and with the projected increase in leisure time, this development looks set to continue and increase. The chapters that follow give some account of other kinds of work in the theatre as well as acting, of a variety of training schemes from drama school courses to degrees and diplomas, of opportunities in companies as diverse as the National Theatre and a group performing on a housing estate, and indicate in passing some of the other ways in which drama has a part to play now and in the future.

Chapter 2
Behind the Scenes

Introduction

You can get some idea of the range and variety of backstage jobs by looking at the small print in a theatre programme. At the top of the scale of employers are the National Theatre of Great Britain which has three theatres under one roof and has 800 full-time staff (including cleaners and catering staff but excluding actors), and the Royal Shakespeare Company, which runs four theatres and is the biggest theatre company in the world.

The current RSC programme has a formidable list of credits: two joint artistic directors, a technical administrator, a general manager, a development administrator, a publicity controller, a production controller, a financial controller, departments covering voice, technical systems, scenic art, scenic workshop, sponsorship, wigs and make-up, property shop, paint shop, merchandising, casting, construction, wardrobe, safety, music, publicity, a company manager, a chief lighting operator, a chief lighting engineer, a chief stage technician, a head of sound, a production manager, a systems engineer, nine directors, six designers, and of course a cast of actors.

The scale is unique; many of the jobs do not exist as separate jobs in other theatres, but on a much smaller scale have to be done by one person; they also arise in television and films.

(Incidentally, if you want to take a look at what goes on in a big company, the National Theatre runs daily conducted tours of the building including the workshops and backstage areas except Sundays. For details see page 103.)

The Producer

This is a job that occurs in the commercial theatre: in a subsidised company many of the duties will be done by the artistic director or administrator.

It's up to the producer to shoulder the economic and managerial problems involved in putting on a play: he will choose the play, rent the theatre (its size will depend on running costs), engage the director and stars, and be responsible for paying all the bills, from the rent, rates and insurance to the salaries of the staff. He has to raise the money to put on the production and if box-office takings fall, decide when to close it.

The money is raised from backers — rather charmingly known also as 'angels' — who are prepared to put money into the theatre because they hope for a good return on their investment, are interested in the theatre, trust the judgement of a particular producer with a good track record. The London theatre attracts American investors as well as film companies, writers, agents, theatre people and businessmen.

Although a producer has to consider his backers, he will also express his personal taste in the kind of plays he manages: Michael Codron, for example, has a reputation for putting on plays of intellectual distinction, while other producers may specialise in farces, thrillers or musicals. You can't train to be a producer as such — some, like John Gale, the executive producer at Chichester, are ex-actors — but useful qualifications include tact, persuasiveness, a sound business sense, a flair for organisation, and a nose for what goes in the theatre.

The Director

He has overall responsibility for the artistic side of a production and must conduct the rehearsals and keep an eye on all the backstage and technical departments involved. In recent years directors like Peter Brook, Peter Hall, Trevor Nunn and Jonathan Miller have become very influential, stamping their style and interpretation on a production and often proving as much a draw as the star performers.

Work on a production starts with the director, who may even have devised the script — as John Barton did with *The Wars of the Roses*, his highly successful version of Shakespeare's history plays — or commissioned it from a writer with whom he has built up a working relationship, such as John Dexter's with Arnold Wesker and Lindsay Anderson's with David Storey. Or it may be a play he has always wanted to direct, and worked on in his mind for a number of years.

Either way he — and most directors are men, though there are one or two women (the late Buzz Goodbody, Gillian Lynne) — will start with definite ideas about the production including who he wants to appear in it (this will have to be worked out with producer and casting director), who he wants to design the sets and costumes, and who he would like to design the lighting. His choice will probably be based on previous experience and on relationships that have been built up over the years, and he will be in a position to get rid of any actors he can't get on with.

By the very nature of the job directors tend to have strong personalities and can be abrasive and temperamental. They are the ideas men of the theatre, and they have to put over their ideas to the company and shape the production during rehearsals. Once a play opens the director's job is finished, and he doesn't have very long to accomplish it — 20 weeks at the National Theatre but often no more than a month in the commercial theatre. During that time he must coax, bully and stimulate the cast into fulfilling his vision, and know how to get the best response from them. Some directors give actors almost complete responsibility for their interpretation, while others have worked out exactly how they want the parts played.

Some directors also take on the extra duties of an

artistic director, which involves managerial work including responsibility for theatre policy, for planning the season's programme and for supervising the budget. Although some directors are part of a company — the National Theatre has resident directors — they are usually freelance, globe-trotting figures, moving from production to production in a way described by Jonathan Miller as 'whoring round the world like a tinker'. They usually receive a fee for each production plus a royalty while it is running, so a long-running success can buy a breathing space and perhaps the chance to undertake an interesting but not well-paid project.

Most directors begin their careers with some experience as actors or stage-managers, though there are now training courses for would-be directors (see page 54). Actor-directors, such as Sir John Clements, Sir John Gielgud and Lord Olivier, are not as common as in the past when the actor-manager was a colourful figure, but other opportunities for stage directors include television and films (Lindsay Anderson), opera (John Schlesinger at Covent Garden, John Dexter at the Met, Jonathan Miller with the ENO, Scottish Opera and Kent Opera), and teaching at drama schools.

The Casting Director

He or she operates in large companies and in television and films and, as the title suggests, is responsible for working with the producer and director on casting a production.

The casting director keeps extensive records of who has done what, and is a natural target for agents trying to get work for their clients. Casting directors go regularly to drama school productions to spot new talent, and are always auditioning and interviewing hopefuls and possibles. The casting director will know who is currently available and draw up lists for the director to choose from, arrange auditions, and work out the financial details with the actors and their agents.

It's a job that involves a certain amount of horse-trading and requires tact, a cool head, and the ability to cope with crises and delicate situations — when an actor suddenly quits a production or turns out to be already committed elsewhere.

The Designer

The sets and costumes for a production are sometimes the work of different designers, especially if it's something large-scale, but more often the same designer is responsible for both. He or she will work closely with the director, interpreting and sometimes helping to shape his ideas, and many designers form close working relationships with particular directors, for example, John Dexter and Jocelyn Herbert.

The designer produces drawings of the sets and costumes for the scenery and costume departments to work from, and also a scale model of the sets which will be explained to the cast at the first rehearsal, when an outline of the set is marked on the floor in tape or chalk for the guidance of the actors until the actual set is ready.

A stage designer needs not only a thorough knowledge of period settings and costumes, but also a sense of style, of what looks effective and exciting on stage, and an ability to work within a budget and adapt to a variety of stage shapes, from the traditional picture-frame proscenium stage to arena and theatre-in-the-round areas.

For suitable training courses see page 48.

Production Staff

In a large company like the National Theatre, which is in effect five companies performing in three separate theatres, there is a series of production workshops each with its own speciality. Although this kind of scale is rare, some of these jobs are found elsewhere in opera and ballet companies for example, and in television and films, and they give a good idea of the scope of production work.

Armoury

This small department is responsible for making armour and weapons such as swords and pikes, for special effects such as gunfire and shells, and for decorative metalwork such as brass items and candelabra. The members of the team tend to be experts — gunsmiths, silversmiths and such like — with a strong interest in period weapons, armour and costume. In smaller companies such equipment is borrowed or hired.

Metal Workshop

Here the heavy steelwork needed for stage shows is designed and manufactured; the National Theatre has three fully qualified welders (see page 76) and an apprentice — the only welder in the country to serve his apprenticeship in a theatre, and chosen from 42 applicants. Their work ranges from making steel supports and complex trees to the huge armillery sphere which hung over the stage at the start of *Galileo*.

Carpenters' Workshop

Technical drawing as well as carpentry skills comes in useful for building sets. The carpenters at the National Theatre do a lot of overtime and pride themselves on the quality of their work. For the staging of *Galileo*, for example, they were asked to build the vast raised disc which was used as the principal playing area and a huge doorway that took two carpenters a week to make and was a solid three-dimensional affair that gave the illusion of a stone arch.

Paint Workshop

This is where the sets are painted and work done on scenery like the carpenters' Roman arch, which was covered with a mixture of sawdust and glue and then with a substance like Polyfilla before being given two coats of paint. Knowing

17

how to create the right textures and surfaces is all part of a scene painter's skill, and the job involves being prepared to cope with the demands of the designer, however exacting or outrageous, and doing last minute work on a set, which may look different when it is lit. Although sets are often kept to a minimum and even dispensed with in many modern productions, in opera and ballet they still tend to be very realistic and massive.

Property Making Shop

Cigarettes, whisky, champagne, glassware and crockery, and lighters are among the things sometimes acknowledged in a theatre programme — and no doubt the props person has fun scrounging them — but in many productions the properties are more elaborate and have to be either specially made or bought.

Props come in for surprisingly close scrutiny from audiences — witness the letters that delight in pointing out mistakes in television programmes — and they have to be thoroughly researched. Property-making skills range from cabinet making to wood turning and upholstery, and there's no cutting corners, as David Allen found when he was given the job of making a throne for the Pope to use in *Galileo*. David had already worked on another production of the play when he was training at Wimbledon College of Art, but that had not prepared him for the six weeks it took to come up with a colour that was finally acceptable to the designer. Another example of the painstaking effort that goes into the job was a grassy mound which involved the whole department in a fortnight of doing nothing but unpicking string and knotting it on a hessian base (see Jim Hiley's *Theatre At Work*). The property shop is also responsible for special effects, such as chairs that collapse and pictures that fall off the wall.

Whether you make or buy properties — or comb the local antique shops trying to persuade dealers to lend that little table that would be just right for Act II — you need an eye for detail, an enthusiasm for research and for tracking down authentic items, from 1920s lighters to Victorian lamps, a magpie instinct for collecting things that may come in useful one day — the National Theatre has drawers of spectacles, watch-chains and other accessories — and a certain inventiveness.

Wardrobe and Wigs

Although costumes are often hired from a theatrical costumiers, a large number are made by the wardrobe departments. The National Theatre has built up a collection of over 11,000 garments, and their wardrobe includes expert cutters who also advise the designers on fabrics and know how they will look and behave on stage. The work requires a good knowledge of period fashion, and at the National they have actually pioneered tailoring pre-1800 costumes in an authentic way. In a company this size the cutters have assistants, and casual help is also used when a new production involves an enormous amount of sewing. Materials have to be chosen and bought — as economically as possible — and they often need to be dyed or treated to obtain a particular colour or special effect. Costumes have to be fitted and altered, and there are all the extras like shoes (usually bought), tights and gloves. Anything special in the way of hats is usually handed over to a freelance milliner, who will also need a good knowledge of different periods.

Accessories can be a full-time job in themselves, with demands for ornate jewellery, orders and chains of office, crowns, tiaras and elaborate masks. Another specialist job is making and looking after wigs, for which a City and Guilds certificate is a useful qualification. The hair is bought and then fashioned as required, and a wig can take several days to make. Beards too can be very time-consuming, as they have to be cleaned and recurled every time they're used.

In a resident company the wardrobe keeps a record of all the actors' measurements. Fittings can be a lengthy business, with actors parading up and down in costumes while there are agonising debates with the designer, sometimes over small matters such as the size and colour of buttons. The work often involves long hours and requires inventiveness, adaptability, and a willingness to accept criticism and cope with the kind of crises that can arise at a dress rehearsal when a director or designer suddenly decides that a costume or accessory simply won't do.

The wardrobe is also responsible for looking after costumes and repairing and cleaning them. This is no small matter with, say, a ballet company, where the performers sweat freely and costumes need frequent washing, and the extensive tours often undertaken by opera and ballet companies involve mountains of packing and unpacking, ironing, pressing, and cleaning.

Make-Up

Most actors learn make-up at drama school and like to do their own, but they may need expert help with extreme changes. Make-up is a highly skilled job in television and films, where so many shots are in close-up.

The Stage Manager

The stage manager and his team are responsible for organising rehearsals and making sure that the performance itself runs smoothly. A stage manager usually has several assistants known as ASMs (assistant stage managers), and a deputy in a large company, and the job requires a gift for handling difficult, temperamental people with firmness and tact, the ability to keep calm in a crisis, an eye for detail, a good memory and, above all, a sense of humour. In small companies an ASM may also be asked to play small parts or understudy, and in the past this often gave actors their first step on the ladder.

It's up to the stage management staff to see that the actors know when they're needed for rehearsals, both by putting up a notice on the call board and, if necessary, giving them a personal call. Rehearsals are organised in consultation with the director, and careful notes have to be made of any script changes, all the moves and actions of the actors, and all the ones relating to scene changes, sound effects, changes in lighting, when to take up or lower the curtain etc. One of the ASMs will have the job of prompting, both during rehearsals and at the actual performances, as even the most experienced actors do sometimes dry up (forget their lines). It's also an ASM's job to keep an eye on the props to make sure that they are available every night, and to arrange with the wardrobe for actors to have costume fittings.

In a large theatre or opera house the stage manager can be in charge of very sophisticated equipment. At the National Theatre, the control box has an intercom system that allows the stage manager to talk via headsets to the stage technicians, lighting and sound people, the musical director, and colleagues in the wings or at the side of the stage. He or she (the National has a female deputy stage manager) can also give verbal and visual (a flashing red light) cues for scene changes, tannoy out into the rest of the building to address the audience and, when the front of house manager gives the OK and the actors are ready, start the action.

The stage crew will include a team of scene-shifters, whose work requires physical strength and split-second timing. Scenery often has to be flown (stored above the stage in the flies), and on an arena stage such as the National's Olivier, where there isn't a curtain, the stage staff have to steal on in the dark to make lightning changes.

The Lighting Designer

The theatre electrician may be in sole charge of the lighting or, in a large theatre with sophisticated equipment, part of a team headed by an expert like William Bundy, Andy Phillips or Richard Pilbrow, who will design a lighting plan for the production. The team will rig the lights, operate them during the performance and deal with any technical problems. Lamps are positioned to show actors in the best light, as well as to achieve sophisticated effects, and in modern theatres the lighting plan can be fed into a computer which activates memorised cues.

The Sound Manager

The job ranges from giving the occasional sound cue (noises off) to providing music if there are no live performers, electronic effects, and solving any acoustical problems. In some theatres the acoustics can be improved by boosting, and sound levels can be adjusted.

The House Manager

The job involves looking after the theatre and supervising its day-to-day running and maintenance. The house manager has to make sure that the cleaning, catering and security arrangements run smoothly, and is responsible for everything to do with the comfort and wellbeing of the audience, from seeing that any broken seats are mended to hiring staff to act as ticket collectors and programme-sellers. The house manager remains on duty throughout the performance and is expected to deal with any complaints or problems that arise. The job doesn't require any stage training or special qualifications, but some experience of working in the theatre would be a recommendation, and being an assistant to a house manager is a useful first step to a career in arts administration.

The Box Office

This, too, makes a good starting place for anyone who aims at arts administration. The box office is in charge of ticket sales both at the theatre itself and by post and through agents. It may operate the traditional system of crossing off seats sold on a seating plan or have a computer that projects the seating plan onto a small screen so that the box office can see at a glance what seats are available. The box office manager is also concerned with promotion and marketing, for hiring his own staff and for checking the takings.

Experience of accounts or general management could be useful.

The Press Officer

Dealing with the press is only one of the functions of this very busy department, which is responsible for everything to do with publicity. Its work is vital, because however outstanding a production, audiences won't come unless they know about it in advance and have had their interest aroused.

Publicity plans have to be made well in advance. They include priming journalists with ideas for articles, persuading surprisingly reluctant directors and actors to be interviewed — many are too busy or mistrust the press — and commissioning a top-flight photographer to do a photosession. (In small theatres the photographer may work for the local paper, or be a regular who has proved dependable.) The pictures are used for publicity displays, perhaps in the foyer, and distributed to the press for use with reviews. These are written by theatre critics who are sent complimentary tickets, usually for the opening night.

The department also has to produce a wide range of publicity material, from posters, advertisements and mailing leaflets to throwaways, cast lists and programmes. Once upon a time these were no more than a straightforward list of credits with perhaps a few advertisements, but nowadays the most simple programmes include photographs and biographies of the cast, while at the top end of the market (the National, the RSC, the ENO, and Covent Garden) programmes have swelled to the size of booklets and include a survey of the historical background to the play, reviews of earlier productions, quotations illustrating the interpretation, and photographs ranging from rehearsals-in-progress to pictures of the author and his friends. They make attractive reminders of the production and tend to be designed by graphic designers and professionally edited. The press office is an interesting opening for arts graduates with a secretarial training.

Tact, self-confidence and a pleasant voice are also useful assets for dealing with the continuous calls from the press, radio and television, and from authors researching books on the theatre.

The Education Officer

Many theatres now have theatre-in-education companies or employ someone to set up links with schools and colleges by organising workshops, talks, backstage visits etc. They may also arrange special schools performances to coincide with O or A level studies and hold career sessions, and this is an area for the drama graduate with teaching or lecturing experience.

Outside the Theatre

The commercial and most subsidised theatres are primarily concerned with drama as a form of entertainment — though it may be entertainment with a social, moral or political message. Outside the theatre, drama is being developed as a tool with a number of other purposes.

The use of drama in schools, aided by the setting up of theatre-in-education companies (see page 92), is intended to help children become articulate and confident as well as to introduce them to an experience that might not otherwise come their way, especially if they have a working-class background or live in regions remote from the theatre. The trend has led to an increase in demand for drama teachers.

Drama as a form of therapy has wide implications: it is now being used to help people cope with problems in a variety of situations, from hospitals to prisons, and is being used also in industry, where trainees are encouraged to act out situations — dealing with employees or difficult customers — as a means of learning how to handle them. All this has potential for those with drama skills.

Another development has been the setting up of arts and community centres with a wide range of projects for all ages including drama workshops where plays are devised to focus attention on current affairs and matters of local interest. Regional arts organisations and festivals are flourishing too, and all these need not only drama advisers but administrators and secretarial help.

Case Studies

Julia's interest in the theatre began as a teenager, when she and a group of friends in the sixth form went to a drama workshop at their local theatre and were fired with enthusiasm by a dynamic teacher.

> This gave me the idea of reading drama at university, and after applying for several courses I was accepted for a drama and French joint honours course at Exeter. The course seemed to have a bias against West End theatre. Instead we were encouraged to concentrate on fringe and community theatre activities, which didn't much attract me. For one thing, the pay was so poor, and I didn't feel the kind of commitment you need to live on a pittance. I had a go at teaching stage management to a group of teenagers, but I didn't find it very rewarding as they weren't prepared to learn and work hard.
>
> I then decided to do a secretarial course and have now got a job in the publicity department of a publishing house. I started as a secretary, but I tried to give the impression that I would welcome responsibility and had ideas for publicising books. I think my drama training has given me confidence, and this is an asset at publishing parties and when dealing with the media. For the future, I've set my sights on becoming a publicity manager.

Kate always wanted to act and went straight for a course at drama school. At the end of the course she couldn't get a job, but she and a group of friends decided to form a small touring company and managed to get backing from a local arts organisation.

> We all felt passionately about women's rights, and devised several plays to put over our views to working-class audiences who wouldn't dream of going to an ordinary theatre. We performed in community centres and church halls, living fairly rough and on a diet that was rich in brown rice, lentils and beans.
>
> We had a real sense of community, and although it was

hard work I really believed in what I was doing. But then after a while . . . I don't know . . . I think I began to have doubts about how effective we were and so did some of the others, and the group broke up.

I tried teaching, but I felt strongly that I wanted to help the less fortunate so I decided to train as a speech therapist. It's a four-year course, but I'm finding it immensely rewarding. My drama skills are very useful and I feel that now I am heading for the right job.

As you can see, the kind of people who study drama don't find easy answers to what to do with their lives at the end of the course. Drama is an open-ended subject with many possibilities, and its justification as training lies in its ability to turn out graduates who are prepared to experiment, to find a variety of uses for their skills, and sometimes even to create the kind of job that really suits them.

Chapter 3
Making an Early Start

Introduction

A delight in showing off, one of the fundamental ingredients of acting, comes naturally to many children. Most enjoy being the centre of attention and saying, 'look at me; watch me.' Some are quick to learn a song, or a dance, or a recitation that they will perform to an audience of proud parents and fond relatives at the drop of a hat.

Most parents take this in their stride, but some, perhaps with secret theatrical ambitions of their own and spurred on by their child's good looks and apparent talent; or because they themselves are in the theatre, or because the child itself wants to go to dancing classes, see these as signs that Justin or Matilda are destined for the stage and decide to encourage them by sending them to a stage school.

Stage Schools

The majority of those offering full-time education (see page 103) are in the south of England; one or two are boarding schools, but there are also a number of schools all over the country that offer part-time training, and unless they particularly want to send their child to boarding school, most parents will probably opt for the most convenient school in their area.

Such schools belong to the private sector of education and come expensive. Fees can be anything from £200 to over £600 a term (around £1,000 a term for boarding

27

school), and most schools have extras such as school uniform and private music lessons. Some local education authorities give grants for dance training, as it is vital for ballet dancers to start their training young, but they are unlikely to be so sympathetic to junior drama training.

Some stage schools take children as young as five, and all like to interview the child to assess its stage potential (older children may also be asked to do a simple audition). The general curriculum includes subjects such as English, French, history, geography, mathematics, art, and religious knowledge, as well as training in drama, voice production, dancing (usually ballet, tap, modern dance and character), mime, singing, and possibly music. Pupils are usually prepared for O level exams, but academic standards may not be as high as in state or public schools, and parents of academically-gifted children should consider carefully the consequences of opting so early for a vocational training that may perhaps make it more difficult for the child to go to university. On the plus side, however, children at stage schools tend to be happy, well-mannered and well-adjusted, and the acting and dancing are good outlets for their energy.

Many stage school pupils don't in the end go on the stage but their training has positive benefits for self-confidence, overcoming shyness and self-consciousness, and enhancing the ability to make a good impression — useful assets in a number of jobs.

Many stage schools, however, have impressive lists of ex-pupils who did make it in the theatre, and also have good contacts with theatre managements and television and film casting directors. They are expert at preparing children for auditions. Some have their own theatres and regularly put on plays and shows to which agents and talent scouts are invited. Some regularly supply pupils for annual shows such as pantomimes and ballets.

Professional Appearances

Not all casting directors are looking for stage-school children, and some may even have a prejudice against them. Ann Robinson, assistant casting director at the National Theatre in London, prefers to recruit children from the Anna Scher Children's Theatre, an amateur workshop group in Islington that stretches the imagination of local children with acting games and improvisation techniques.

When the National were looking for a boy to play the young Andrea in their production of Brecht's *Galileo*, they chose 13-year-old Marc Brenner, a boy who had no ambitions to be an actor but just happened to be rehearsing for his local youth club play when an agent who was looking for a boy to play a concentration camp victim telephoned. Marc went along and was wrong for the part, but the agent noticed his similarity to the actor who was to play the adult Andrea and sent him along to the National. He read for director John Dexter — and was offered the part.

Many directors prefer the freshness and spontaneity of children without any formal training, and the Royal Shakespeare Company often needs boys to play pages or princes. Luck plays a major part in landing such roles, and children often hear of them through friends, teachers or contacts in the company. They are usually engaged for one production only, which is put on at intervals throughout the season, and paid a small fee of around £10 a performance. Children are also sometimes needed to walk on in opera performances — in London, this usually means Covent Garden and the Coliseum — and are usually recruited from ordinary schools.

Such opportunities may be the start of an interest in the theatre. The excitement of the backstage atmosphere and the kind of 'high' that comes from appearing in front of an audience can kindle theatrical ambitions.

Musicals and TV programmes requiring children often advertise in *The Stage* — and there is no shortage of applicants. Children from all over Britain arrived by the coachload to audition for a recent series on Channel Four. The auditions themselves were shown on television and they included some ear-splitting moppets, little boys who told jokes, and song and dance routines in styles ranging from Shirley Temple to Elvis Presley. Many of the children sang inappropriate love songs, but however unsuitable the material, self-confidence and personality shone through.

Legal Restrictions

The hours and conditions under which child performers work are strictly controlled by local authorities, who will license only a limited number of performances per year and who make sure that school work is not seriously affected. Children are carefully chaperoned backstage, and seen safely home after the performance.

Equity

Regular child performers may qualify for a temporary Equity card that will entitle them to full membership when they reach 16 without having to do the usual probationary work in the provinces.

School Drama

Drama is now an important part of the school curriculum, but the aim is not to produce actors so much as to help children gain self-confidence and self-esteem. Drama classes tend to concentrate more on improvisation techniques which encourage children to use their imagination and to express themselves, than on producing full-length plays. However, the end-of-term play, often by Shakespeare, remains an enjoyed and respected ritual in more traditional schools, and many actors from John Gielgud to Simon Ward made their first appearance in a school play.

Some schools also do drama as CSE and GCE subjects. The CSE drama examination includes written and practical work including improvisation, either alone or in a group, and a prepared piece of dramatic work.

The GCE courses include O level drama, O and A level drama and theatre studies, and A level theatre studies.

Written work (questions on set plays and theatre history) is balanced by creative projects and a practical test of dramatic skill either solo or as part of a group.

O and A level courses in drama and theatre studies (and in other performing arts GCE subjects) are available for students over 16 at a number of colleges of further education and tertiary colleges. For an up-to-date list see the latest edition of the British Theatre Institute and DATEC Directory of Drama courses in higher education.

As yet O and A levels in drama are not as highly regarded by universities as more academic subjects, but polytechnics and colleges of higher education are more willing to accept them as entrance qualifications for drama degrees and courses with theatre elements.

Theatre Workshops

Many provincial and repertory theatres and arts and community centres now run workshops aimed at encouraging young people to express themselves and develop an interest in the theatre.

Typical of such events are the various workshops organised by the Greenwich Young People's Theatre, which take place in the evening and on Saturdays and cater for a wide range of age groups. The 7-9s can play creative games, make things and do projects involving music and drama: there is a drama workshop for the 11-plus, a modern dance workshop for the over-14s, a chance for the over-16s to communicate through art, music and drama, and sessions for photography and sound-recording. The cabaret group explores 'a variety of songs in a variety of styles — looking at how they came into being and what comments they made on their society, as well as performance technique'; the session builds up to an informal cabaret evening.

Team leader John Cockett stresses that the idea is not so much to produce items of performance standard as to develop self-awareness and use improvisation as a means of exploring themes and ideas relevant to the lives of those taking part. This may result in a formal script, perhaps

31

written with help from an experienced writer, and built up into a performance.

This kind of involvement in live theatre is proving very popular, and there are similar workshops all over the country. If you'd like to find out more about them, the places to look are in theatre programmes, on school notice-boards, in your public library, and in the local press. Young People's Theatre schemes are also listed in the *British Alternative Theatre Directory* and *Contacts*, or you can write to the National Council of Theatre for Young People for details. There is usually a small charge for taking part. Greenwich, for example, have an annual subscription of £1 plus 15p per session; there is no subscription and only 5p a session for the under-11s.

The Royal Court Theatre runs an interesting scheme to encourage young playwrights, who are invited to send in scripts for a Young Writers Festival; this is held around Easter, when entries from all over the country are performed in the Theatre Upstairs.

The National Youth Theatre

A more traditional introduction to theatrical experience is offered by the National Youth Theatre of Great Britain, which was started by Michael Croft in 1956. A former actor turned schoolmaster, Croft found himself in charge of the school play at Alleyn's School, Dulwich, and transformed rather precious Shakespearian productions into exciting events involving hundreds of pupils, many of whom would never previously have dreamed of taking part.

The NYT celebrated its Silver Jubilee in 1981, and it has had to fight hard to establish itself as a permanent theatre group. Initially it concentrated on Shakespearian productions, which were staged in the West End, the provinces and abroad. The 1960 *Hamlet* (which included Hywel Bennett as Ophelia, Michael York as Horatio and Simon Ward as Rosencrantz) was invited to the Theatre des Nations in Paris, and the 1961 *Julius Caesar* was acclaimed at the Berlin Festival and in Italy. Croft also set up a working relationship with playwright Peter Terson which brought the company specially written plays that gave a new insight into the lives of working-class young people; the concern with contemporary themes was continued by Barrie Keefe, who started as a schoolboy member of the company.

The NYT started life as a holiday activity, but it soon developed into a new movement of theatre by young people for young people. The Arts Council eventually recognised its importance and gave it a grant (withdrawn in the cuts of 1980) and in 1971, after the failure of a scheme to set up a permanent Youth Theatre Centre, the London Borough of Camden offered the Shaw Theatre in Euston Road as a permanent base for the company. This has enabled the NYT to do more new and commissioned plays in its summer seasons while continuing to stage one or more Shakespearian productions a year.

Although the company doesn't see itself as a drama school but as an opportunity for young people to stretch themselves and experience high standards of teamwork and discipline, it has produced a remarkable crop of young actors and actresses. Former members include Simon Ward, Helen Mirren, Hywel Bennett, Timothy Dalton, Derek Jacobi, Diana Quick, John Stride, Michael York, Robert Powell and many others. It has also given experience to young stage designers and technicians; former members are now working in the stage management, lighting, sound and wardrobe departments of national companies, reps, opera companies, films and television. Some have formed their own lighting companies, and one has set up an international trucking company that specialises in the technical needs of the entertainments industry.

The NYT has also had a strong influence on drama teaching; former members have gone on to teacher training colleges and to study drama at university before becoming drama teachers or working in theatre-in-education teams.

Membership

The company is open to anyone between 14 and 20, and every year between three and four thousand young people apply to join. You don't need any educational qualifications, but you're not eligible to join if you're already at university or drama school, or working in the professional theatre. Those who join while still at school can stay on until the upper age-limit even if they become full-time students.

The summer season courses have places for about 500, and you will need to apply in February (you should check the exact date, which varies slightly from year to year, and the application fee). All applicants are interviewed; if you want to act you will need to prepare two speeches, one from Shakespeare and one from a modern play. Those who are interested in stage management, workshop, scene painting, wardrobe, lighting, sound and administrative work may have to provide samples of their work or evidence of their interest. The audition itself is not the deciding factor; what the company is looking for is a lively personality, the ability to work well in a team, and the will to 'put in long hours on a difficult job'.

Interviews are held in London, Aberdeen, Belfast, Birmingham, Bristol, Edinburgh, Manchester, Newcastle, and Swansea, and successful applicants are interviewed again in late May or June. The courses themselves take place in London, and although the fees are modest (normally around £30), you will also have to find the cost of travel and board and lodging, which you must arrange for yourself. In the past some local authorities have made grants to help with these expenses, but this area has been much affected by cutbacks.

Courses

The annual NYT programme includes four courses.

1. A full production course that includes training in improvisation, voice production, verse speaking and mime,

and culminates in full-scale productions and studio presentations in London theatres.

2. Two-week technical courses in stage management, set construction, lighting, sound, and costume. At the end members then work on a production in the department in which they have shown the most promise. (There is no fee for technical courses.)

3. Special two-week junior (14-16) courses in mime, movement and voice production, with strong emphasis on improvisation. At the end of the course, members put on an entertainment they have devised themselves.

4. Senior courses for older applicants, who get the same instruction as in the full production course plus the chance to work on experimental or studio productions that are presented privately to invited audiences and may later go into the NYT repertory.

For details apply to: The General Secretary, The National Youth Theatre of Great Britain, Shaw Theatre, 100 Euston Road, London NW1 2AJ; 01-388 0031.

Chapter 4
Vocational Courses

Introduction

In the past getting into the theatre was a much more chancey business than it is today. For example, in his autobiography *A Postillion Struck by Lightning* Dirk Bogarde describes going past the Uckfield Theatre one day and just wandering in to ask for a job painting scenery. He was paid a shilling an hour to do odd jobs such as painting flats, manhandling furniture, screwing the handles on a chest of drawers, and spent all his spare time and weekends helping. Eventually he was offered a part at five shillings a performance, and although the play itself was a disaster, it confirmed the youthful — he was then about 20 — Bogarde's ambition to go on the stage.

With no formal training and virtually no experience Bogarde auditioned for the Old Vic and somehow managed to get through his three 'well contrasted pieces' under the dauntingly cold eye of the brilliant director Tyrone Guthrie. Much to his surprise he was offered the traditional beginner's role of spear carrier, with the possibility that he might also be one of Romeo's friends. His resolution to become an actor was strengthened by meeting an enthusiastic young actor with 'a shock of wild hair, bright eager eyes and wild gestures' who told him; '. . . you have to be totally dedicated. Totally. Nothing else will do here.'

The young Peter Ustinov's advice to Bogarde is still sound, but today no young untrained actor would be taken on by a major company — least of all in London, where

Equity rules forbid the use of beginners. Forty years on, the acting profession takes training far more seriously, and the old method of walking on, making the tea, prompting, and being a general dogsbody now comes *after* full-time training, and the likelihood of a company taking someone straight from school or university is not high, especially with so many drama-school graduates competing for the all-important Equity cards.

National Council for Drama Training

If you are sure that acting is your goal, rather than some other career allied to the theatre for which a degree might be more useful, you will need to go to drama school. This is the method of training recommended by the Gulbenkian report *Going on the Stage*.

Among other things, the Gulbenkian report was concerned about the standard of drama-school training and the existence of a large number of inferior schools. To combat this and help to ensure that students receive the kind of training best suited to equip them for the professional theatre, the National Council for Drama Training was set up in 1976.

The NCDT sees the accrediting of acting courses as its first priority, because it helps to raise the standard of drama training, gives local education authorities useful guidance in reaching decisions on student grants, promotes closer links between the profession and the training sector, and should make entry into the profession a smoother process. In this last connection, agreement has been reached with Equity to reserve a certain number of Equity cards for the graduates of accredited courses.

The first list of accredited courses was published in 1980; recognition applies to the course not to the school as a whole. One-year courses are not accredited, and neither are some of degree or degree-equivalent status because the NCDT didn't feel they offered the most suitable training for students wishing specifically to become professional actors.

All the schools with accredited acting courses are listed on page 105 and described in the Conference of Drama Schools prospectus. The Conference, which played a leading part in the formation of the NCDT, stresses that its 17 member schools have in common 'the determination to preserve the highest possible standards of professional training' and recommends prospective students to make a preliminary choice of at least three schools and then study their individual prospectuses. There are, of course, many other drama schools up and down the country, but before settling on one that is not a member of the Conference you should look carefully at the curriculum, the facilities it offers and — a useful guideline — at what has become of former students. If none has made the grade with a reputable organisation, you may not either.

Drama School Curriculum

Most acting courses are for three years, at the end of which the college awards its own diploma. The content and emphasis of the courses varies from school to school, but the aim is the same: to teach students to use their voice, body and imagination.

In the first year students concentrate on learning how to breathe, how to project their voices and how to move, and may also have classes in singing, stage fighting, mask work, improvisation, and stage makeup. In the second year they may learn tumbling, acrobatics, more dance styles including tap and jazz, and begin rehearsing for public performances. There will be lectures and seminars on social history, the history of drama and the visual arts, with the aim of ensuring that students are as much at home in Elizabethan tragedy or Restoration comedy as in a modern play. Modern plays can make surprising demands on actors: in a recent production at the National Theatre the cast had to perform on a cabin cruiser that was literally afloat on the stage.

Most schools have their own theatre — some more than one — and put on productions in a number of styles.

Students get a chance to show what they have learned in full-length productions, and these are particularly important in the final year, when agents and casting directors are looking out for the most promising students. Students are also given audition practice, and most schools provide training in radio and television techniques, some in specially equipped studios.

Choosing a School

This will be influenced by a number of factors, and although it will come down to which school is willing to offer you a place, it's worth taking a careful look at what the schools offer and expressing some initial preference.

Do you want to live at home or breakaway and assert your independence? Is there a school in some place where you've always wanted to live? London may seem attractive if you live in the provinces, but it can be very expensive — one prospectus suggests that it could cost in the region of £250 a month for living expenses.

Are you attracted by any particular technique, such as the Method approach to acting? This is based on the ideas of the great Russian teacher Stanislavski and is taught exclusively at the Drama Centre in London NW5, though other schools use some of Stanislavski's ideas.

Do you like the idea of working with a particular company? The Bristol Old Vic Theatre School has close links with the Bristol Old Vic, while the Guildhall School is based in the new Barbican complex, which is the London home of the Royal Shakespeare Company.

As well as listing the courses and facilities available, a school's prospectus will give you some idea of the particular flavour of the school.

The rather austere prospectus of RADA for example, with its plain gold cover, is in keeping with its very conservative, rather arrogant reputation — it was founded in 1904 and boasts a most impressive list of former students.

In contrast, the East 15 Acting School's striking, colourful prospectus suits its creative, progressive approach.

Founded in 1961, the East London school explores and develops the methods and techniques of Joan Littlewood's Theatre Workshop, and you can get some idea of whether it would suit you from your response to its policy:

> We believe that the greatest actors are nurtured in a group of give and take and talent. If you do not give you will never receive. If you have no talent we cannot acquire it for you.
>
> We believe in discovering reality before harnessing it to theatricality. We must understand the truth of life and living before we presume to act it.
>
> We base our training on the uniqueness of the individual and his or her ability to change, adapt, extend, perceive, accept and reject.

There's lots more along these lines, and students are encouraged to relive their childhoods, collaborate in writing plays and documentaries sometimes based on taped interviews, and rediscover the animal joy of living by outdoors exercise that includes climbing trees. This is a school for the more unconventional student who wants an experimental approach to theatre.

The Drama Centre's Method approach combines the teaching of Stanislavski, Grotowski and Brecht, and the ideas of Rudolf Laban, the architect of European Modern Dance. The Method involves trying to get inside a character by considering the background of his or her life and developing imaginative insights into his or her relationships. The student is invited to look beyond the actual text and to study, for example, Hamlet's relationship with his dead father, his mother, his friend and his mistress. The intellectual nature of the training is underlined in the account of the movement psychology class which:

> . . . employs exercises, a technique of relaxation and improvisation to help the actor raise to consciousness and control the forces that determine the expressive qualities of movements, gestures and speech. It investigates the basis of characterisation and examines the way in which the physical relationships that the actor sets up as he moves among people and things within the volume of the stage reflect the conflict within.

Different again is the Rose Bruford College's community theatre arts course which aims to create new drama for new audiences. Shows for a wide variety of audience take place in all kinds of places from community centres to the open air, and use words, movement, actions, images and music to comment on and celebrate life.

Students take part in tutorial classes on body, voice and musicality, study groups, performance workshops and community assignment tours. Recent course productions have included an original musical for young people on TOPS schemes, a play about contemporary homelessness that toured community centres, a preschool show and a pub show performed on a GLC overspill estate, and an all-women production of Brecht's *Threepenny Opera*.

The Drama Centre makes the point that a large number of prospective students never ask themselves what they need to learn or what they expect a school to provide, and recommends you to try and find out what the various schools are like and what distinguishes one from another. This may not be easy, but it's a good idea to send for lots of prospectuses, read up about the theatre — do you know who Stanislavski was, if not see the book list on page 111 — look through the theatre file at your local Job Centre library, meet some actors and actresses and ask them about their training, and try and talk to some of the students when you go for an audition.

Most acting courses take between 20 and 30 new students a year, and the more reputable schools can afford to be very selective, so you'll be wise to apply to a number of schools.

How to Apply

Write to the registrar of any school you are interested in asking for a prospectus and an application form. The prospectus gives details of the school's premises, its policy and courses, and its entrance requirements and fees.

Most drama schools have a minimum age limit of 18 (17 in one or two cases) and an upper limit of 25, 26, or

30 at the most.

Some schools have no specific academic requirements but others want some GCE passes — usually 5 O levels or 2 A levels.

The application form will ask for details of schooling and any theatre experience, as well as the usual information about age, height, etc. Some may ask for a passport-type photograph, referees, such as the head of your last school or college, and you could also be asked for a doctor's certificate to say that you are fit enough to take part in what is regarded as a very strenuous profession.

Courses begin in the autumn term; you need to send in your application form by early spring at the latest — each school has its own terminal date.

Auditions

These can be quite an ordeal, so try and get in some practice — perhaps by taking a speech examination. It's important to be able to do your best when it counts, as the panel will be judging your actual performance and won't be impressed by excuses.

Each school has its own audition requirements, but they tend to follow a basic pattern. At the Guildhall School, for example, applications have to be in by the end of October and preliminary auditions are held in December. The audition takes the form of a short movement warm-up and improvisation followed by an unprepared dance routine. The candidate then performs three contrasting pieces of his or her choice, one of which must be from a comedy and one from Shakespeare, each lasting not more than three minutes, and sings a short song. Those asked to come back again for a weekend in January or February do more detailed work on their audition pieces and improvisation before a panel that includes members of the Royal Shakespeare Company.

Preliminary auditions for the Bristol Old Vic School take place between the beginning of November and the end of April. Candidates have to prepare a short piece from a classical verse play (preferably by Shakespeare) and from a modern prose play, and are also asked to sing a short unaccompanied song. Hopefuls are invited to a weekend school in Bristol, which allows the staff to work with them before making a final choice.

This kind of two-tier audition is typical. Bear in mind that as well as an audition fee, auditions can also involve travelling expenses and the cost of overnight accommodation. Fees range from £7 for the Central School to £12 for LAMDA and £19.95 for the Guildhall School, and are non-returnable even if you don't turn up (unless you have a very good reason, such as illness or bereavement), so you can tot up quite a bill if you go for several auditions.

Choosing the right audition pieces is important. Don't be too ambitious, and try to be realistic about the type of actor or actress you are. If you have a natural flair for comedy, for example, make the most of this rather than choosing a straight speech for which you may be physically and temperamentally unsuitable. You'll do far better in a speech you feel at home with.

Fees

Drama training, like other forms of further education, is expensive. Fees vary — and are usually higher for overseas students — but for 1982/83 the majority were over £2,000 a year, to which have to be added living expenses.

Grants

Owing to cuts in local authority budgets, the grants position is unclear. While grants for degree courses are mandatory (which means if you are offered a place you will get a grant), those for vocational drama courses are discretionary (which means that the LEAs are not obliged to make an award and the exact amount of any award may depend on their opinion of the school and the course). You are unlikely, however, not to get financial help if you are offered a place on an accredited course, though priority is given to longterm residents in the LEA area and you will usually need to have lived there for at least three years. In some areas it is also difficult to get an award if you are over 25.

Ideally, your grant should cover approved fees (which are usually paid direct to the school) and maintenance, which includes the cost of accommodation, travelling expenses, necessary books, equipment etc. The maintenance award is usually based on the income of the student's parents, and is paid to the school at the beginning of each term. Payment is sometimes delayed, and students are advised to make sure that they have sufficient funds to see them through the first few weeks.

Application forms for awards can be obtained from your present school or college or from your LEA, and are available from January onwards for the following academic year; your form should be returned by June at the very latest (for some authorities it is earlier) if you plan to start a course in the autumn term, but there is no need to wait until you have been accepted for a course. Applications are dealt with in the order in which they are received, so it is in your interest to apply as soon as possible. It is important at this stage to make sure that your chosen course will really equip you for the career you have in mind, as discretionary awards are usually only for first qualifications. A degree in drama or theatre arts may not provide the best training for a would-be actor, and some authorities might be reluctant to fund a further year at a drama school.

Many schools have awards and scholarships set up to honour distinguished former students, so if you do have trouble in getting a grant, they might be prepared to help.

Grants for postgraduate study are discretionary, but some courses qualify for bursaries or studentships from the Department of Education and Science. The Arts Council Training Section awards bursaries for a variety of training schemes for designers, directors, performers, technicians and stage managers, but such schemes are for professionals who have already had two or three years experience in the theatre.

The booklets *Getting a Grant*, *Grants to Students* and *Guides to Grants — Postgraduate Awards* should be available at your school, local library or careers office.

Stage Management Courses

Most acting courses include a certain amount of practical stage work, but there are also a number of specialised courses for prospective stage managers.

Most courses don't have formal educational requirements but candidates are asked to attend an interview. The kind of qualities looked for include a high degree of intelligence, practical ability, artistic flair, a sense of authority, tact, an obvious enthusiasm for the theatre and some experience of backstage work, perhaps on school or amateur productions.

The National Council for Drama Training has accredited stage management courses at the following schools:

Bristol Old Vic Theatre School

20 places are available on a two-year course that covers every aspect of theatre work including stage carpentry, lighting, sound, technical drawing, welding, photography, slidemaking, production management, box office, front of house management and administration. The course prepares students for technical work in the theatre, radio or television. Students share facilities with the Bristol Old Vic, and have the chance to work under professional conditions.

Central School of Speech and Drama

16 to 18 places are available on a two-year course for students who want to become stage managers or specialists in lighting, sound or some other department of backstage work. First-year studies include theatre history and repertoire, learning how to build scenery and make properties, the use of stage, lighting and sound equipment, sharing some classes with acting course students to understand how actors work, and helping with student productions. Most of the second year is spent working as a stage manager or as head of a production department on plays presented in the Embassy Theatre or Studio, or

45

elsewhere, under professional directors.

Guildhall School of Music and Drama

In the first year of a two-year course students have classes in stagecraft, technical drawing, design, lighting, sound, scene-painting, property-making, play study, score reading, the history of the theatre, costume and history of art, voice, movement and makeup, so that by the end of the year they have a sound working knowlege and understanding of the theatre. During the second year the emphasis is on practical work, including television, and students get the chance to work with professional companies and can specialise in an area that particularly interests them.

LAMDA

The two-year course, run jointly with Theatre Projects Trust Ltd — a group of companies actively involved in technical activities in the professional theatre — aims to give students a practical working knowledge of the technical aspects of the theatre and good all-round training for potential stage managers. The first year includes acting classes, the preparation of prompt scripts, company management and planning, production management, and practical work on drama course productions, as well as lighting design, scene design, sound and effects, the history of the theatre, and studio management in broadcasting and television. Students selected for the second year do more responsible work on the Academy's productions and wherever possible in the professional theatre.

Mountview Theatre School

Intensive lecture and class work is followed by a variety of practical assignments in connection with the 40 productions staged every year in the school's two theatres. Students work as stage managers, lighting and set designers, operate sound and lighting equipment, make properties and build and paint scenery, and they also get the chance to work as apprentices in professional theatres throughout the country.

Rose Bruford College of Speech and Drama

12 places are available on a two-year course that includes

practical experience of stage management, lighting, sound, costume and wardrobe techniques, scenery construction and handling, properties, and stage mechanics. Students in their second year take greater responsibility for mounting and running productions, which range from fully mounted productions in the college theatre or in London to theatre-in-education, community and mobile theatre presentations.

Royal Academy of Dramatic Art
The four-term course covers all aspects of stage management and touches on lighting and scenic design. Students progress from stagehands to deputy stage managers, and study a wide range of subjects including the history of furniture, period costume, sound recording, and business management.

Royal Scottish Academy of Music and Drama
The one-year technical certificate course provides training in the technical aspects of theatre and television and includes stage carpentry, lighting, stage management, camerawork, floor-management and vision mixing.

Two other members of the Conference of Drama Schools have stage management courses that are not accredited:

Guildford School of Acting and Drama
This practical two-year course gives students experience of the day-to-day problems they are likely to encounter in their professional career, as well as the technical background. The construction, technical and managerial aspects of the school's many productions form a basis for their studies.

Welsh College of Music and Drama
The design/stage management course gives students the opportunity to learn the practical skills involved in stage presentation. They include stage management, lighting, staging techniques, sound, set design, scenery construction, costume design, make-up and wig care, and a short course in radio and television. Students are encouraged to specialise, and have the chance to work on a wide range of productions.

Theatre Design Courses

Design courses are currently being assessed by the Art and Design Committee of the Technical Education Council (DATEC), and approved courses will award TEC certificates and diplomas.

Scene painting and design are included in stage management courses, but there are also one or two specialist courses:

Bristol Old Vic Theatre School

Four places are available each year for students with the basic qualifications to do one or two years' specialised training covering every aspect of practical design, scene painting, property making, technical drawing and model making, with plenty of practical experience through the school's public productions. The one-year course is open to Dip ADs and graduates of university drama or fine arts departments; Pre-Dip AD training at an art school is required for the two-year course.

Croydon College

The three-year course for the Higher DATEC Diploma is designed for students who want a career as setting, costume or lighting designers, design assistants, production managers or technicians, and sets out to equip them with a comprehensive range of skills.

Students must be over 18 and have passed in at least 5 O levels, or completed a recognised foundation course (the equivalent of sixth-form study), or hold a DATEC Diploma in Three-Dimensional Design or its equivalent. Exceptions may be made for gifted students with theatre experience. The course is eligible for an LEA mandatory award.

Subjects studied during the first year include textual analysis, set and costume design, lighting techniques, production management, model making and technical drawing, scene painting, property making, cutting and making costumes, the history of the theatre and the performing arts. Students are assessed at the end of each term, and have usually decided on their special interests by the end of the second term. They are then streamed into setting and costume studies or lighting and production.

During the second year students work on a series of projects that include mounting a minor production in a studio theatre, a major exhibition project, and a full-scale production with a visiting theatre company. The college has close links with the Ashcroft Theatre, the Croydon Warehouse Theatre and the Croydon Youth Theatre. The 1982 Workshow included sample sets and costumes for *The Admirable Crichton* designed for the Chichester Festival Theatre, *La Cenerentola* for the Glyndebourne Festival Opera, and *The Wicked Cooks* for the Lyric Theatre, Hammersmith; students were responsible for the design, construction and painting of the sets, and for buying and dyeing fabrics, and cutting, sewing and decorating the costumes, while the lighting and production management students supervised the layout, rigging and lighting of the exhibition. There was also an exhibition illustrating the history of stage lighting, a puppet performance, and a slideshow featuring productions on which the students had worked.

By the third year students are firmly established in their areas of specialisation and spend the autumn and spring terms working as assistants to professional designers, as design or technical assistants in regional theatres, and in workshops and workrooms. They return to college for the summer term to work on a final assessment project set by an external examiner.

Croydon College also offers a one-year postgraduate course for mature students who have already done an art and design course or drama training, or spent at least 12 months in the production department of a professional theatre. The intensive course covers set, lighting and costume design, and students are expected to work on five theatre design projects set by distinguished outside designers. The final assessment is by an external examiner at an interview.

Guildhall School of Music and Drama
There are three places on a one-year course for students who want to make a career of scene painting. They also study set design, lighting, scenic construction, stagecraft and technical drawing.

In addition there is a theatre design course lasting one year with ten places for postgraduates. Entry is by interview and there is a minimum age of 21.

Royal Academy of Dramatic Art
Designers who have completed a full-time course in theatre design can do a four-term course in scene painting and design that includes the mechanics of handling and rigging, laying in and marking out, modelmaking, groundplans, working drawings, painting and texturing, budgeting and ordering. Students work with professional directors on half a dozen public shows.

Slade School of Art
A two-year full-time postgraduate course in theatre design leading to a Higher Diploma in Fine Art.

West Sussex College of Design
Two full-time two-year courses in theatre/TV design and crafts leading to a DATEC Diploma in 3-D Design and an Advanced College Diploma.

It seems appropriate to mention here also, rather than in the next chapter, four degree courses leading to a BA Hons awarded by the CNAA (Council for National Academic Awards, see page 108).

City of Birmingham Polytechnic
Three-year full-time course at the School of Theatre Design that includes practical experience of working with local theatres and companies.

Central School of Art and Design
Three-year full-time course.

Trent Polytechnic
Twenty places are available on a three-year full-time course allied to the Nottingham Playhouse. The emphasis is on

practical experience — students are expected to act in the costumes they design — and ends in the design and presentation of a public performance.

Wimbledon School of Art
Thee-year full-time course.

Theatre Wardrobe Courses

Bristol Old Vic Theatre School
A one-year course covering all the practical aspects of wardrobe work including maintenance, hire, buying, dyeing and printing, pattern cutting, costume making and wig care. Prospective students should have a basic knowledge and practical experience of dressmaking.

Guildhall School of Music and Drama
There are three places on a two-year course in prop-making.

Mabel Fletcher Technical College
A three-year course in theatre wardrobe.

Wimbledon School of Art
A two-year course in theatre wardrobe.

Technical Courses

The Association of British Theatre Technicians' policy when giving careers advice is 'not to encourage those contemplating a job in theatre but to point out the many hardships to be encountered in theatre work, and to seek to discourage all but the committed from pursuing a theatre career'.

That said, ABTT deal with an increasing number of enquiries and have produced a pamphlet, *Training for the Theatre*, that gives details of the courses they have helped to set up for scenic carpenters, theatre electricians and theatre sound engineers.

Croydon College
A one-year day-release course for stage technicians who are currently working in the professional theatre. There are

no entry qualifications and students are given time off to attend classes. The course aims to extend the students' knowledge of aspects that may not be covered in the normal work situation.

Paddington College
A full-time one-year course, largely college-based but with some time spent in a theatre. The course is for young people without professional experience, but applicants should have an active interest in the theatre and provide some evidence of their ability to study technical subjects. Selection is by interview and the course qualifies for an LEA discretionary grant. Mature students may also qualify under the TOPS scheme.

The course covers electrical craft theory, electronic principles and sound equipment, and theatre studies; trainees are attached to various theatres in and around London as members of the theatre's electrics department.

There is also a two year day-release course for electricians already working in the theatre. There are no entry qualifications and students are given time off to attend classes. The course is designed to increase basic technical knowledge and covers principles of electrical installation, electronics and sound, and theatre services.

On completion of both courses trainees sit for the City and Guilds Theatre Electricians examination.

ABTT has also cooperated with Paddington College in a one-year course designed for those interested in sound in the theatre. It follows the general lines of the Electronic Servicing course with additional work on sound and acoustics, and subjects studied include electronic systems and signals, electronic components and equipment, audio systems and acoustics, and theatre techniques. Trainees get direct experience by a system of attachment to various theatres where they serve as members of staff. Applicants should be at least 16, have some O levels or CSEs, and provide some evidence of an interest in the theatre and sound. The course qualifies for an LEA discretionary grant, and mature students may also qualify under the TOPS scheme. Successful trainees are awarded a college certificate and can continue their studies on an appropriate City and Guilds course.

Hammersmith and West London College

A full-time one-year course for scenic carpenters that concentrates on all aspects of scenery building and contains a considerable amount of practical work, much of it done in the scenic workshops of professional theatres. Subjects studied include craft theory and practice, technical drawing, science and calculations, theatre subjects and communications skills, and the practical use of tools and machinery. Applicants are required to show evidence of practical aptitude, have a potential for studying technical subjects, and give some evidence of an interest in the theatre. Students may be eligible for an LEA discretionary grant. At the end of the course trainees sit for City and Guilds examinations in communications and calculations and are awarded a college certificate.

Royal Academy of Dramatic Art

Two specialist diploma courses of four terms each giving practical training under repertory conditions. The stage carpentry course includes bench work, handling and care of tools, knowledge of timber, hardware and canvas, building, erecting and maintaining sets, the mechanics of scene handling, rigging etc, working drawings and groundplans, budgeting and ordering. The stage electrics course starts with basic backstage work including scenery handling and flying, and continues with all aspects of lighting and sound, and work on public shows with professional directors.

Applicants must be at least 19 and should have some practical knowledge, though they don't need any formal academic qualifications. Selection is by interview.

All these courses are in London. There is apparently not a sufficient number of applicants to justify setting up courses elsewhere. Technicians in regional theatres, however, can usually find an appropriate course at their local technical college, and there are grants to help with the cost of attending day-release courses. Some theatres also run apprenticeship training schemes for which bursaries are available. The training normally lasts for two years, and electricians are required to take the Theatre Electricians City and Guilds examination.

Both ABTT and the Arts Council make awards to those already working in the theatre who wish to broaden their experience, perhaps by working at other theatres or undertaking individual projects.

Directors' Training

Directors need practical experience of the theatre, and often gain this by working as actors or stage managers first. Many drama schools also provide useful training on their stage-management courses, and the Central School of Speech and Drama recommends its stage-manager course as providing 'a foundation for those who aspire to become directors'.

Four students a year aged over 21 are accepted for a special three-year course for directors, linked with the actors' training, which is offered by the East 15 Acting School.

A degree course can also be useful, especially if it involves a knowledge of the history and background of drama, the social and political conditions that have influenced it, the theatre of other countries and cultures, and experience in studying and interpreting texts. The most important qualification, however, is a lively, inventive, imaginative intelligence, no matter how it has been trained.

One of the most admired directors of recent years, Jonathan Miller, trained as a doctor and was drawn into the theatre through his involvement as a student with the Cambridge Footlights. Miller's interest in psychology has strongly influenced his work for the theatre, television and opera, but his failure to set up the ideal conditions under which he would like to work has made him decide to return to medicine as a university professor. His example would be hard to follow — there are few polymaths around

— but he illustrates the level of intellect that flourishes in a director's role.

Regional Theatre Trainee Director Scheme

Financed by the Independent Television companies, this scheme is intended to help men and women between 20 and 26 who want a career in theatre production and direction. It is advertised in *The Stage* in January, or you can write direct (see page 107). Application forms have to be returned by the first week in February — there is no grace for late-comers.

The form asks for details of your theatre experience and allied interests as well as what play you would like to put on as your first production, why you want to be a director, and what plays you have seen in the last year, with a brief comment on one. Applications are sorted by an interviewing panel that sees shortlisted candidates in March; some are chosen for a further interview where representatives of the theatres take part. There are usually three places, and appointments are taken up in the following autumn.

The training lasts two years — the second year depends on the trainee making sufficient progress. Trainees are paid a modest salary (£4,394 per annum in 1983) by the theatre company they are working for, which receives a grant from the television companies for this. The trainee works on productions with the artistic director, and also spends time in the stage management department, workshops, electrics, wardrobe, box office and accounts, so that he or she gains an overall knowledge of the problems, particularly financial, involved in running a theatre. Trainees who show sufficient ability are given a production of their own in the first year and guaranteed a minimum of two productions in main or studio theatres in their second year.

You're not guaranteed a job at the end of the course, but former trainees include film director Ken Loach, Trevor Nunn and three other directors of the Royal Shakespeare Company, directors of a number of regional repertory theatres including the Birmingham Rep, the

Derby Playhouse, the Nottingham Playhouse, the Citizens Theatre, Glasgow, and the Thorndike Theatre, Leatherhead, as well as the Head of Drama at Hull University and a number of freelance producers, directors and writers.

Arts Council Bursaries

The Arts Council's Directors' Scheme helps promising directors at different stages of their careers.

For young directors, there's an award to help them study all aspects of directing, including the artistic direction of a theatre or opera company for a year or possibly longer.

Awards are also made to experienced directors who have not been responsible for the artistic direction of a theatre, to enable them to be appointed associate director at a theatre for a period of up to a year.

The third type of award covers in-service training for directors who have already had some directing experience in the professional theatre or opera and want to extend their knowledge of specific areas of work in this country or abroad.

Details of the scheme are available from the Drama Director of the Arts Council.

Case Study

Caroline worked on a number of student productions while she was studying drama at university, and by the time she got her degree she knew that she wanted to become a director.

> I realised that first of all I needed some direct experience of working in the theatre, and I was lucky enough to be taken on as a production assistant by a rep where they needed help backstage and on the administrative side. After directing my first professional production and working in another rep, I decided to apply for an Arts Council bursary because I wanted to work at the Bristol Old Vic. I found the interview very exacting and was delighted to be one of five successful candidates.
>
> Bristol was a whole new experience with so much to do:

reading new scripts, assisting on several main productions, and working with the students at the theatre school. I found working with young people particularly rewarding, and organised a series of children's workshops that proved very popular. I also began to find my feet as a director, first with two lunchtime productions and then with a fullscale production that was well received. I was asked back for a second year and am now establishing workshops for the 14-18s on a regular basis as well as doing more work with the theatre school. I have been promised at least one more major production which I hope will help to establish my reputation as a director.

Chapter 5

Degree Courses

Introduction

A number of universities and institutes of further education offer degree courses in drama and theatre arts. They are mainly concerned with drama as an academic subject, and although many of them provide opportunities for practical stagework, their aim is not primarily to train students for a professional stage career. This is not to say that some degree students don't end up on the stage but they usually need further training at a drama school first, and it can be difficult to get an additional grant to cover this. So if the stage is your immediate goal, you should think twice before embarking on a degree course.

Arts degrees are not in themselves a direct training for any particular profession. They are intended rather to develop the mind by intellectual disciplines so that a graduate can tackle a wide range of jobs that require intellectual skills. But drama does have a surprising number of practical applications including, of course, the obvious career of teaching, and is increasingly becoming a subject in its own right with many openings for specialist drama teachers.

An academic qualification in drama can also lead to jobs in arts administration, recreation management, public relations, theatre management, publishing, and on the management side of films, radio and television. There is keen competition for such jobs, but once you have found your way in, it is likely to be less precarious than a career on the stage.

So a degree course may be right for you if you are seriously interested in working in the theatre or in a way of life somewhat allied to it, and are not sure whether you have quite enough talent and charisma to succeed on the stage.

Entrance Requirements

You need to have some natural bias towards academic study and an interest in reading round a subject. Are you, for example, interested in social history? Do you enjoy finding out more about the life and work of your favourite authors? Do you know anything about theatre history? Have you enjoyed studying plays for O and A levels? Have you a favourite playwright or type of play, and do you like going to the theatre — yes, are you actually prepared to spend money supporting it? Do you like performing or are you more interested in helping to stage your own interpretation of a play? Do you like reading about the theatre — or writing about it? These are some of the areas that will be explored by a drama course.

There is keen competition for places and you will need a minimum of five GCE passes, two of which must be at A level. The most useful A levels are likely to be English literature and a foreign language or a subject such as art, history, mathematics, or a science. No special preference is given to O or A levels in drama or theatre studies.

Applications for admission must be made through UCCA (Universities' Central Council on Admissions); ask for details on how to apply from your school or write direct.

Courses

There is no such thing as a typical drama course, so it's a good idea to write for a number of prospectuses and give yourself time to study them and make further enquiries — are any old pupils of your school studying drama? — before deciding which ones to apply for.

Some courses are very academic and offer little training

in practical skills such as voice, movement, acting etc, while others concentrate on performance and performance skills. Most drama departments have their own theatre or drama studio, and some also have facilities for learning about radio, television and film work.

Teaching usually takes the form of tutorials (small informal groups that meet once or twice a week with a tutor), seminars, lectures and practical classes, and you'll be expected to write essays and take written examinations.

Drama can be studied as a single honours subject occupying the main part of the syllabus, or combined with one or more subjects, for a BA (Bachelor of Arts) or B Ed (Bachelor of Education) degree. Degree courses are available at universities and at some polytechnics and colleges of higher education, where a comparable degree is awarded by CNAA (Council for National Academic Awards). While not directly vocational, CNAA courses tend to be more practical. Unless otherwise stated, all courses are full-time and last three years.

University Courses

Birmingham University
The drama and theatre arts course involves studying the text, performance, design and production of plays, theatre history and dramatic literature; plus practical work in voice, movement, improvisation and elementary acting techniques, and technical projects. The amount of practical work in the second and third years depends on the student's talents and interests. The course in music, drama and dance is based on the same principles but concentrates on the relationship of the basic elements. Drama can also be linked with any other subject as part of a combined course.

Bristol University
The study of European drama centres on texts and performance and includes quite a lot of practical work. Students also study the language of the visual media, and options for specialised study in the second and third years

include social and ritual theatre, American theatre, practical film, and practical television. Drama can also be studied in Joint Honours schools in combination with English, a modern language, music, or Greek.

Exeter University

Instead of lectures, drama is studied through studio-based projects that aim to develop each student's physical and theatrical resources as well as the intellectual abilities. The skills of the creative actor who works outside the professional theatre are encouraged, and there are opportunities for working with the Northcott Theatre. Drama can also be combined with English or German.

Glasgow University

The course studies the nature and tradition of drama and practical work gives students an insight into the arts, theatre, and dramatic literature. The two-year course in film and television studies includes practical television work in the second year. Under the Scottish Teachers' Regulations graduates can become specialist drama teachers after a further one-year course at a college of education.

Hull University

A two-year study of the art of theatre is followed in the third year by four compulsory topics and a wide range of options linking dramatic literature and theatre history. The Special Honours course gives the chance for creative work on individual playwrights, genres and styles. Drama can also be studied jointly with a number of other subjects. Courses include practical experience of acting, dance, mask work, improvisation, directing, stage design, stage management and front-of-house organisation, technical theatre, film-making, radio and TV and theatre-in-education, with regular productions in the studio theatre.

Kent University

Courses are academic rather than vocational, with some training in theatre skills for specialised honours and drama major students. Theatre studies range from the Greeks to the present day, and include aspects of plays in performance.

Lancaster University

The course studies many forms of theatre including Stanislavski, Brecht and popular theatre, and provides basic performance skills as well as expecting students to concentrate on particular aspects of theatre. The department has the use of the Nuffield Theatre studio and stages some public performances.

London University

Goldsmiths' College: courses in drama with English, French or German include dramatic literature and theatre history from its classical origins to the present day together with practical experience of acting, directing, design and stage management. Particular aspects of English, European or American drama can be studied in-depth, and there are opportunities for specialised practical work. Facilities include the George Wood Theatre, three drama studios, workshop, design studio, and wardrobe and sound room.

Royal Holloway College: single and combined honours courses range from the theatre of the Greeks and Japanese to the present day, with emphasis on plays in performance. Students are asked to review plays and films, and take part in practical theatre work such as fullscale productions and workshops. There are classes in acting, directing and stage management, and single honours students attend two vacation courses with a drama school or theatre company. Specialised options include a director's course, television and radio drama, music and theatre, and film. The college has its own studio theatre.

Westfield College: the drama plus language course, run in collaboration with the Central School of Speech and Drama, covers the history of drama from its classical origins to the present day and includes the practical study of speech and movement, styles of dramatic presentation, and actor-audience relationships. The wide range of special options includes the in-depth study of English, European and American drama. Drama may be combined with English, French, German, Greek, Latin, classical studies, or

Spanish, and the prospectus stresses that courses are not a training for either teaching or the stage.

Loughborough University
The drama course recognises the essential nature of drama as a group activity and gives equal weight to academic and practical work. Students have opportunities for creative and experimental work and take part in productions. Drama can also be combined with English.

Manchester University
All courses cover the history and development of the theatre from its origins to the present day. Practical work includes speech, movement and vocational performance courses, and basic courses in stage crafts. Third-year students can choose from courses in performance studies, theatre-in-education, design, theatre criticism, and contemporary film. Practical work is done in the Stephen Joseph Studio and in the University Theatre. Drama can also be combined with English, German or French (four-year courses), or Italian or combined studies (three-year courses).

Surrey University
Vocational courses in the first and second years, run by the Guildford School of Acting, equip students for careers in drama and dance, particularly in the social field, and explore the effects of new technology on public performances and on film, television, and the other media.

Wales University
Aberystwyth, University College of North Wales: the history of European theatre and dramatic literature is combined with a basic training in acting and technical skills. In Part 2 students choose some areas for more intensive study and continue acting if they have shown sufficient talent. There are two major productions each term as well as experimental and fringe activities. Drama can also be combined with another arts subject.

Bangor, University College of North Wales: the course includes a general introduction to ancient and modern drama and practical work in voice, movement and improvisation. Drama can also be combined with a number of subjects including English, modern languages, classical studies, Welsh and sociology.

Warwick University

The theatre studies course concentrates on the theatre of the last hundred years and includes some practical illustrative work. The combined courses with English, French or Italian include one theatre course in each year and look at dramatic theory and criticism, theatre history, and twentieth-century avant-garde theatre. The theatre studies and dramatic arts course consists of seven academic courses in the Department of Theatre Studies and five more practical drama courses in the Department of Creative Arts.

B Ed courses, some lasting four years, are available at Cambridge, Durham and Exeter.

CNAA Courses

Bulmershe College of Higher Education

BA and BA Hons in Combined Studies. The course combines critical and creative activities and there is discussion and practical work on plays and films.

Crewe and Alsager College of Higher Education

BA and BA Hons in Combined Studies. The creative arts course includes textual study, movement, design and performance. Students are encouraged to follow up their own interests. Contemporary innovations and original work are explored in the third year.

Dartington College of Arts

The four-year BA Hons theatre course is geared to theatre language and communication through presentational or interactional theatre. Students study the relationship between acting, movement and writing, and are encouraged to develop a special interest in an area such as music, design, folk studies, therapeutic drama, or the performing arts of India or Japan. The third year is spent in an urban area working in a school, hospital, factory or community centre where the student is concerned with the particular needs of the locality.

Huddersfield Polytechnic
BA Hons in Humanities with a drama option. Drama can be studied as a major subject in the second and third years, or a second-year drama major can be followed by drama as a single subject in the third year. Students study the academic and practical aspects of performance, with emphasis on the relationship between text, design and mime, the links between society and the theatre, and the various ideas of the scope and function of a play. There are in-depth studies of major periods, and project and performance work in a studio setting.

Leicester Polytechnic
BA Hons in Performing Arts. The practical and theoretical study of drama is related to dance, music and arts administration.

Middlesex Polytechnic
BA and BA Hons in Performance Arts. Basic skills in dance and music are required for a course that involves the aesthetic, technical and historical aspects of theatre, acting, voice, movement, improvisation and interpretation, current theatre practice and performance, and the entertainment needs of the local community. Drama is one of the options available on the BA/BA Hons Humanities course.

Newcastle upon Tyne Polytechnic
BA Hons in Creative Arts. Practical work is used to develop creative and practical insights. The historical and critical studies concentrate on nineteenth- and twentieth-century drama, and third-year students can specialise in acting, directing or playwriting.

Trent Polytechnic
BA Hons in Creative Arts. Drama is one of two options for two years and includes the history and literature of drama, performance skills and techniques, and an examination of

the relationship between drama and the other arts through critical studies and practical workshops. There are outside speakers and performers and visits to performances and exhibitions. Third-year students concentrate on twentieth-century drama and practical projects.

Wales, Polytechnic of
BA Hons in Humanities. For the first year, drama is part of a foundation course in the humanities. In the second year it can occupy half the course and is studied along with two other subjects. In the third year drama can be the major subject, with a minor interdisciplinary course. Courses in TV and radio, including the preparation and presentation of scripts and theoretical study, are part of the BA Hons in Communication Studies.

Winchester, King Alfred's College
BA Hons in Drama. The theatre and television studies course presents a historical perspective and looks at contemporary work. The final year includes a course in practical theatre and television skills that involves students realising a text and/or dramatic theme through both media. Drama can also be combined with English or History.

For B Ed courses and others with drama components see the CNAA *Directory of First Degree and Diploma of Higher Education Courses* and the BTI and DATEC *Directory of Drama Courses in Higher Education.* Rose Bruford College (page 41) also has a BA Hons in Theatre Arts course.

Colleges of Higher Education Courses

Bretton Hall College
BA Hons, University of Leeds. Drama and creative arts courses include improvisation, mime, dance, acting, directing, stage techniques, textual study, playwriting, practical dramatic criticism and history of theatre. Students carry out individual and group projects, with fieldwork in Stratford, London and Bristol.

Chester College of Higher Education
BA Hons, University of Liverpool. Combined studies degree including drama with two of the following: art, biology, computer studies, literature, ecclesiastical history, French, geography, history, music, maths, PE, religious studies, psychology, liberal studies in science.

Ilkley College
BA/BA Hons in Performing Arts, Recreational Studies, Humanities, Community Studies, University of Bradford. For the performing arts course, students are encouraged to combine dance, drama and music within the framework of the theatre in order to develop their own abilities through design and composition projects, practical work in the community, and work in the professional theatre. Facilities include dance, music and drama studios, a sound resources studio, video equipment and workshops. Other courses have drama options.

Liverpool College of Higher Education
BA/BA Hons, University of Lancaster. Creative and technical practical work is considered most important and there are regular productions in the studio theatre. Students get opportunities to explore and experiment in movement, improvisation, the play in performance and closed circuit television presentation; they also study the literary, historical, critical and theoretical backgrounds of the drama and theatre.

Nene College
BA Hons in Combined Studies, University of Leicester. Drama is taken with other subjects in a modular degree. Textual and historical studies are combined with practical work which seeks to explore areas of personal interaction, group dynamics and the problems of group management, playwriting and improvisation. Third-year drama studies concentrate on twentieth-century theatre.

Nonington College
BA in Performing Arts, University of Kent. All students do a course in theatre and performance studies and can choose

67

drama, dance or music as main or subsidiary subjects.

North Cheshire College
BA in Theatre Studies, University of Manchester. First two years include practical and performing theatre skills, dramatic literature, and theatre and media studies. In the third year students concentrate on the theatre today and have the opportunity to work in the professional theatre on the management and technical sides.

Ripon and York St John College
BA/BA Hons, University of Leeds. Modular courses in which students can specialise in drama, film and television, dance and movement, or group together elements from each of these areas. The aim is a balance between practical and academic work, and gives great flexibility of choice.

Roehampton Institute of Higher Education
BA, University of London. Academic and practical work are combined in a course that includes improvisation, mime, acting, directing, stage and theatre techniques, and textual study. Second- and third-year students have a range of practical and academic options.

Rolle College
BA in Combined Studies, University of Exeter. Theatre arts course.

Trinity and All Saints' College
BA/BA Hons, University of Leeds. For the first five terms students study drama and English, with an extra drama option from the second term onwards. Drama can then be combined with public media, management sciences (planning and administration), or education, and some time is spent with organisations relevant to the student's interests.

Note: For postgraduate courses at drama schools, universities, polytechnics and colleges of higher education see the BTI and DATEC *Directory*.

Chapter 6

Finding Work

Introduction

So term's over, you've finished your training, and the sky's the limit — or is it?

The lucky students in your year will already have got jobs that will enable them to become full members of Equity (see page 95), and the prizewinners and gold medallists may have been taken on by agents who are now trying to launch their careers. But if you're the average newly-graduated drama student, you're probably wondering how on earth you're going to land that all-important first job that will bring you — if nothing else — experience and contacts.

Contacts

You've probably already realised during your training how important contacts are: the theatre is a vast grapevine, with word of mouth the most popular and effective way of passing on work. You may be a budding Gielgud, know you're just right for the RSC or the National, have the looks and manner for West End comedy, but no one will beat a path to your bedsit. This is no moment to drop friends and acquaintances because they've got work and you haven't and hate moping around trying not to look envious. Keep up with everyone you've ever known, *especially* if they look like being successful. Haunt any pubs where you know theatre people congregate, accept any invitations and think twice before turning down overtures — the director's girlfriend does have a head-start — and above all keep your ear to the ground. If you do hear of likely work, make for the nearest phone and go after it at once. The theatre is a fiercely competitive jungle and no place for modest little violets.

There are also some practical ways in which you can make yourself known.

Photographs

You're going to need a lot of these as you'll have to send at least one every time you apply for a job — and you probably won't get them back. It's not worth going to an expensive photographer: all you need is a reasonably attractive, lively image that does you justice and doesn't look too posed. Maybe you have a friend with a talent for photography. If not, look in *Contacts* (see below) or *The Stage* and get several quotes. Some photographers offer special discount rates for students. A basic session will cost around £30, and postcard-size reproductions work out at around 30p each.

Spotlight

One of the most useful things you can do with your photograph is insert it in *Spotlight*, a bumper four-volume directory of actors and actresses in which everyone advertises. It comes out annually (actors' vols in April, actresses' in October), and the current (1983) cost of a half-page advertisement is £57.85 (including VAT) and of a quarter-page £31.35 — slightly less if you use the same photograph in subsequent years and they don't have to make a new plate. Newcomers need to book space and submit photographs well before the press dates of 1 April for actresses and 1 October for actors.

Entries are listed under various categories — leading and younger leading, character, younger character, and juvenile and juvenile-character — and include height, colour of eyes, telephone number or agent if you have one, and any relevant qualifications such as fluent French and German, dialects, competent horseriding; some people list outstanding or recent parts too. You can include anything that you feel is relevant and eye-catching, and there's no need to be modest — the whole thing is an exercise in self-advertisement. *Spotlight* is used by casting directors in every medium — and yours may be just the face they're looking for.

As well as the casting directory, *Spotlight* also offers advertisers and subscribers an advisory service and keeps up-to-date computerised records of some 40,000 actors and actresses which are referred to at the rate of about 500 telephone calls a day. Such records are particularly useful when parts have to be recast or taken over at short notice. *Spotlight* will put enquirers in touch with you and are in some respects like a vast agency — with the advantage that they don't charge commission.

They also publish *Contacts*, an invaluable guide to people and services in stage, television, screen and radio. This is the place to find the addresses and phone numbers of agents, all kinds of theatre companies from regional to children's, alternative, community and fringe, drama and dance schools, recording studios, film and television companies, as well as tax consultants, photographers and companies who will hire out anything from a claret jug to cowboys and indians costumes and trained birds.

Letters

You'll have to write quite a lot of these when applying for interviews and auditions and should be prepared for disappointment, as probably only a third will get replies and some of these will be turndowns.

Most job advertisements ask for a CV (*curriculum vitae* — Latin for your lifestory) or details of your experience, so it may be worth setting out the basic details — age, height, weight, colour of eyes and hair, special gifts (fluent French, clog-dancing, dialects, good singing voice, expert piano or horseriding, handy at fencing or whatever), drama school or other training, experience so far — in a clear way, and getting some copies run off. It's also useful to photo-copy any reviews — if they're at all impressive. Send a personal letter with your details and photograph, and if it's a company or part you're particularly keen on, say so and why. It could help to distinguish your application from all the others. Some ads ask for a stamped addressed envelope and it's always worth enclosing one: even if the answer is no, it will at least put you out of suspense.

The Stage

This weekly newspaper, which calls itself 'the shop window of the profession', has several pages of job advertisements covering all aspects of the theatre from actors, actresses and stage-managers to electricians, costume designers, wardrobe staff, prop makers and artistic directors, wanted for all types of companies all over the country. There are sometimes advertisements for television and film extras, and it's also a useful source of fill-in jobs while you're resting (see page 80).

Professional Casting Report

This weekly guide to who's doing what is sent to subscribers by post every Monday at a cost of £10 for five weeks. It provides information (some of it rumour) about forth-coming productions in the theatre, television, films and commercials, with detailed casting and audition news. New subscribers also get the 'Who's Where' and 'Who's Who' of Casting Directors to help them track down those who make the casting decisions — wherever they're hiding. The same company also produces *Castingdex*, a list of contact names in television and radio commercials, filmlets and photo-graphy; and *Filmlog*, a monthly guide to feature movie-making in Britain and films with English soundtracks in Europe or with a London casting base, with advance details of casting directors, producers, directors, PMs, addresses, telephone numbers, locations, dates and studios.

Agents

Although some actors prefer to remain in direct control of their careers, most are glad to be able to hand over the business of finding work to an agent.

Agents don't charge a fee as such, but take a percentage (normally 10 per cent) of their clients' earnings, so they are not prepared to take on anyone they don't believe in or feel they can't 'sell'. Anyone can set themselves up as an agent — it's not difficult to get a licence — and agents range from the really big boys like London Management, who have hundreds of clients, to individuals who rely on their flair and contacts to place a handful of handpicked actors. Small agents can offer individual attention and may really get to know their clients and enjoy shaping their careers, while large agents may be more impersonal, with different people handling theatre, films and TV, none of whom may know the client well. Large agents, however, do have considerable advantages: they will probably handle superstars and get to know of forthcoming productions well in advance, giving them the chance to suggest some of their humbler clients for the smaller parts; some also have close links with management, perhaps belonging to the same group.

Ideally, what you want from an agent — apart from plenty of work — is the feeling of being handled by someone who is concerned to build your career. This means not only getting you work, but advising you on what parts to turn down, however tempting they may sound, because they won't help your image in the long run.

Agents also fix the fees, ensure that their clients get proper billing, and represent their interests in any dispute with managements. Fees are normally paid to the agents, who deduct their percentage before paying their clients, so it's as well to make sure that the agent you choose — and who wants you — is financially sound and will pass on any earnings as promptly as possible. Be suspicious of anyone who is too eager to take you on — unless it's a name you recognise or is vouched for by friends. It may seem flattering to be wanted — and it's a great psychological boost to be able to refer to 'my agent' — but it's basically a business arrangement, and needs to make business sense on both sides.

Auditions and Interviews

Even an agent can only put you in the way of getting work by arranging an audition or interview — whether you land the part depends on you. It is also possible, once you have had some experience and got an Equity card, to send your details and photograph to casting directors — perhaps at the National, the RSC, the BBC or ITV companies — and ask for an audition. They will probably see you, unless they are very busy, and although you may not land a part straight-away, they will have you on record should a suitable part turn up.

You will probably have had some training for auditions at drama school and settled on one or two well-rehearsed pieces that show you at your best. At interviews, they want to see and talk to you, often about money. Try and find out something about the part(s) you are auditioning for — if it's a repertory company, see what they're doing at the moment and what the forthcoming season will include. You may then be able to tailor your piece to their style. They will also be looking for someone who they think will fit in and prove a useful, adaptable addition to the company. It's a case of 'if your face fits . . .', but if you don't get the part it could also be a blessing in disguise — something much better may turn up next week.

At some auditions actors are asked to read a part at sight and given only a few minutes to look through the script. Don't be afraid to ask questions: you'll make a better attempt at the part if you have some idea of what's going on and what's expected of you. If you're auditioning for a musical — or a part that includes a song — you'll be expected to sing (and possibly dance too), so go prepared with a number you really enjoy.

Casting directors tend to be non-committal at the time

— they want to see everyone else before making up their mind. If you feel sure you haven't got the part because you were off-form, or made a hash of the reading, put it down to experience. You're going to have a lot of auditions in your career, and the more practice you have, the better.

Contracts

When you do finally get a job, you'll be asked to sign a contract, which is a legally binding document that needs to be taken seriously.

The offer of a contract drawn up under conditions laid down by Equity is the first stage in getting an Equity card, so tell them, get your provisional card, and ask them to make sure that the contract is in order. You should, of course, read it carefully yourself, as it will set out the conditions under which you are offered the part — you may also be required to help with stage-managing or understudy various parts (and you'll want to know which) — and it could also commit you to staying with the company for the rest of the season or the whole of the run. This may seem a wonderful idea when you're out of work, but there could be drawbacks — that casting director you auditioned for six months ago suddenly calls up with a part in a TV serial — and as breaking a contract can be difficult and expensive, it's important to understand how far you are committing yourself.

If you have an agent, he or she will keep the contract; if it's in your keeping, make sure it is somewhere safe where you can find it easily.

Backstage

Agents and auditions are the concern of actors, but finding backstage work also calls for nerve and initiative. It is an area in which the formula a-course-plus-a-diploma-equals-a-job by no means applies. Although most backstage workers have had some form of training, it was not usually with the theatre in mind, and there is a certain amount of prejudice and scepticism backstage about the value of theatre-oriented courses and a feeling that it's a job you learn by doing it.

It is still true that one of the best ways of getting backstage work is by going along to a theatre and knocking on the door. Carpenters, scene-shifters, scene-painters etc are often glad of the extra hand and more impressed by obvious enthusiasm and a love of the theatre than by academic qualifications. The mateyness of backstage life and working together in crews, disposes those in charge to take on newcomers they like and feel will fit in. There are many entrances to backstage work, and persistence and determination pay off.

Case Study

Sylvia Starshine (she adopted this name to help her in her other career as a science fiction illustrator) is an example of the kind of unconventional route that can lead backstage. An American, she was one of the first women in the United States to train as a welder during peacetime.

> I came to Britain because I was interested in archaeology and wanted to work on the reconstruction of an Iron Age farm. Finding myself short of money, I looked for ways to use my welding skill and applied for a job in the metal workshop of the National Theatre, where I was taken on by Eric Dunn, who himself had learned welding in the army. I am now part of a team that is responsible for structural metalwork; my interest in the past also comes in useful sometimes — once I taught an actress how to spin.

Sylvia didn't learn welding in order to work in the theatre, but the skill made her suitable for the job, just as a skill in dressmaking or millinery could lead to work in a theatre wardrobe.

Administrative

Here again determination and commitment count for a lot. An arts degree may be useful in the long run, but on its own it will not get your foot in the door. A head for figures, secretarial training, typing, driving (regional arts associations cover wide areas) are all useful skills, and once you are in a company or arts association there are good prospects for promotion.

Some London secretarial agencies specialise in media jobs, and they are advertised in *The Times*, *Daily Telegraph*, *Guardian* (there is a creative and media appointments section on Mondays), *The Sunday Times*, and in weeklies like the *New Statesman*, *Time Out*, and *The Stage*.

The Training Section of the Arts Council produces a monthly list of arts vacancies which they will send to anyone who supplies stamped addressed envelopes (size approximately 9 x 5 inches).

It is also a good idea to write to any companies or arts organisations for which you would particularly like to work, as you could be lucky and strike a moment when a suitable vacancy has occurred. It's important not to express just vague interest but to set out clearly what you would like to do — work as a secretary, help in the box office, deal with publicity etc — and to list any training/experience/skills that are relevant.

Festivals provide an excellent opportunity for getting short-term experience and are often glad of extra help, particularly at a fairly menial level. They have the added advantage of taking place all over the country, and you can check up on them in the Arts Council's list of Festivals in Great Britain.

Graduates (and non-graduates) who have some experience of arts administration can broaden their knowledge at training courses held at the City University's Centre for Arts and Related Studies. Details are available from the City University or from the Arts Council, who hold regular informal open meetings to discuss arts administration courses and careers.

Chapter 7
Resting

Unemployment is such a common experience in the theatre that the profession has coined its own word for it: the splendid euphemism 'resting'.

Being out of work is not confined to the inexperienced and the unsuccessful. All actors, except those under contract to one of the national companies as associate artists, live from show to show, and even *The Mousetrap*, now in its thirty-first year, will close some day. So even when you do get your first break, or make your first appearance in the West End, it won't mean an end to days of waiting for the phone to ring, weeks of having to convince yourself that you're still an actor.

Case Study

Ian left drama school four years ago and thought he was off to a good start when he landed a job in a rep he admired. The season gave him valuable experience and led to a couple of parts in television and an appearance in a feature film.

> It wasn't the kind of part made for stardom, but it gave me the chance of working on a filmset, which I enjoyed though I prefer the theatre. I missed the reactions of a live audience, and I felt nervous about having to repeat the same sequence again and again because of some detail that was nothing to do with my performance. You never knew which take would turn out to be the real thing.
>
> There were gaps in between my television and film work, but I felt much more confident after the film because I now had quite a useful list of credits. But it was followed by a

frightening period of resting – sometimes I wondered if I'd ever work again. Although I am now on tour in a play that may transfer to the West End, I reckon that in my first four years I have been unemployed for 74 weeks – well over a year.

A friend who left drama school at the same time and has appeared in four West End musicals reckons that she has been out of work (sorry, resting) for 60 weeks, so the question is not *if* but *when* you are unemployed, what can you do?

Cash Help

The most immediate problem, apart from boredom, frustration and depression, is likely to be lack of money, so what government benefits are you entitled to?

If you have been in work and paying National Insurance contributions, you will be entitled to unemployment benefit if you have paid at least 25 contributions in any one tax year, though you need 50 Class 1 contributions to qualify for the full standard benefit. It's important to go to your local unemployment benefit office (listed in the telephone directory under Employment, Department of) on the *first* day you are unemployed, otherwise you may lose money. You'll find that they are quite familiar with the peculiar circumstances of the acting profession.

You may also be eligible for supplementary benefit, which is not dependent on insurance contributions but is means-tested. It is intended to bridge the gap between the money you have coming in and what you need to live on, and it may be worth claiming it if your income after paying rent is less than about £26 a week, and you don't have savings of more than £3,000 (after November 1983). To claim supplementary benefit, get form BL from the unemployment benefit office. You may also be entitled to free NHS dental treatment, free NHS glasses and free NHS prescriptions, as well as a number of other benefits and help with heating and housing costs. The DHSS leaflet FB2, *Which benefit? 60 ways to get cash help*, is a useful guide to what is available and how to make a claim.

Finding Work

Regard your situation as a temporary setback — like landing on a snake in snakes and ladders — and go back to chapter 6. Stir up all your old contacts and make sure that everyone knows you're available. If you have an agent, trust him to do his best for you and leave him to get on with it, but make sure he knows how to contact you as soon as possible if anything turns up. If you have a temporary job, give him a phone number where you can be reached — or the number of a friend or relative who will take a message for you. It may be worth paying to have calls transferred to another number, or using a telephone-answering service such as Message Minders, who have a special rate for Equity members and will take messages for just over £1 a week. Another solution is to buy or rent a telephone-answering machine that will record messages for you. There are some relatively inexpensive ones on the market, but it's a good idea to ask any friends who have one about their drawbacks as well as advantages.

Temporary Work

If nothing seems likely to turn up at once — and waiting for work can seem like the watched kettle that never boils — you might be better off trying to earn some money, though this could affect your entitlement to benefits.

Temporary work needs to be something you can give up at a moment's notice, and preferably with an employer who will be sympathetic if you want time off for auditions. It is also useful if you can arrange to continue paying income tax on Schedule D (see page 98), as otherwise your employer will have to deduct tax at the emergency rate until he receives your correct coding, which means that initially you will be paying more tax than you need to — and at a time when every penny counts.

The Stage regularly has advertisements for temporary

work suitable for resting actors and actresses. Recent jobs have included: canvassing, in-store demonstrators, telephone sales, driving, cleaning and babysitting.

They're none of them likely to be particularly rewarding, either in terms of job satisfaction or easy money, but they could keep you financially afloat and give you an excuse for not lying in bed feeling sorry for yourself.

Fares can eat into earnings, so it's worth looking round for work in your immediate vicinity. Your local paper might give you some ideas. Are there any shops that could do with an extra hand, cafés which are short-staffed, pubs or hotels in need of help behind the bar? Do you live near any exhibition sites or conference venues that might need stewards? Extra staff are also often needed on a seasonal basis: at the seaside during the summer, in department stores and the post office at Christmas. And what about the jobs you did as a student? Are any of these still available?

Useful Skills

Casual work is usually not well paid and it can be very useful to have other strings to your bow. If you have gone straight to drama school you won't have had time for any other training, but if you have any skills or talents, this is the time to develop them.

One skill it's worth paying to acquire is typing. You can learn in the daytime or at evening classes, and courses are run by local education authorities and by a variety of commercially-run schools who often offer intensive crash courses. Jobs involving typing on electric and manual typewriters, as well as audio-typing, are handled by secretarial agencies or through newspaper advertisements.

You may also want to learn shorthand, but this is a longterm undertaking, especially if you want to learn Pitman's shorthand, which uses special symbols. The Speedwriting system, which uses letters of the alphabet, is quicker to learn and claims that you can attain a speed of 100 words per minute within a couple of months if you take an intensive course.

Typing is also useful if you have any kind of literary talent. Few people can write a publishable novel (and, unless you're Jeffrey Archer, the financial rewards are likely to be disappointing), but there is a small but real market for women's magazine short stories. If you fancy your chances, study several issues of the magazines you're aiming at, make sure your story is an appropriate length, and send it typewritten (no one will bother to read anything handwritten) to the fiction editor. Don't waste time trying to find yourself a literary agent — they won't be interested in trying to sell the odd short story. Try if possible to capitalise on your own experience — the misadventures (particularly romantic) of friends, suitably disguised, can make very good copy.

Your drama training may have involved script writing and if you were any good at it and have an ear for dialogue, you could try writing a play, perhaps for radio or television. The BBC Radio Drama Department is responsible for over a thousand broadcasts a year and relies entirely on freelance writers. It receives about 200 scripts a week, so don't expect an immediate answer. It helps your chances if your script looks professional, and the Drama Department has produced some Notes on Radio Drama that outline general requirements and include brief points about the art of writing for radio and advice on methods of submission and layout.

It is also possible to sell the occasional article to a magazine or newspaper. Interesting copy could result from some aspect of your training or theatre experience that would appeal to the general public. Much depends on your skill with words, imagination, and ability to see the potential of a story, and if you do have a flair it should become easier to sell your work once you have found a few sympathetic editors. Provincial papers are more likely to be interested at first — the competition in Fleet Street is cut-throat. The *Writers' & Artists' Yearbook*, published annually by A. & C. Black, is a useful guide to the whole writing scene. It includes advice on writing for newspapers, magazines etc, marketing a play, writing for television, along with a comprehensive directory of names and addresses from publishers to television companies.

A quite different talent that can also be exercised on an occasional or part-time basis is cooking. If you are thinking of hiring yourself out to cook dinner parties for rich friends — and hopefully their friends, too — it could be worth doing a Cordon Bleu course to add a touch of finesse to your native skill.

Other jobs that lend themselves to the personal approach include hair-styling, window cleaning, decorating, driving and removals.

Morale Boosting

Apart from keeping a roof over your head, the other problem with being unemployed is loss of morale. It's not just your bank balance that goes down but your self-respect and, if you're not careful, your appearance. You find yourself making innumerable cups of coffee — and having the odd biscuit or chocolate bar each time — and the lithe You who used up your energy worrying about your part and often didn't find time to eat properly, has become a plump, pasty-looking individual.

Don't let yourself go. Keep in trim by signing up for a dance or exercise class — there are lots around. Apart from safeguarding your figure, you'll benefit from doing a class with other people. Keep mentally trim by catching up on your theatre homework, the background reading you don't normally have time for, the plays you've been too busy to see — and not only the West End successes but some of the more unusual, out-of-the-way shows that extend the range of the conventional theatre. If you live in or near London, *Time Out* will clue you up on what's going on. Practise some of the parts you'd really like to play.

Being unemployed is a real test of how much working in the theatre really means to you.

Case Study

Stella left drama school more years ago than she likes to admit to, and by now she knows she'll never get a really big break. Over the years she has had a number of minor parts on stage and done quite well in films and television, where she exploited her long dark hair and slightly foreign appearance.

> Nowadays it's mostly crowd work, and I depend increasingly for my income on my shorthand and typing. If I gave up acting altogether, I could get a full-time secretarial job with paid holidays and other perks, but I prefer to work as a temp for an agency that accepts that I may be unavailable at short notice. It sounds crazy, but I find I can get through the most boring work because I don't feel that it's my real job. Something else may turn up at any minute, and then I'm back with the kind of people and the kind of atmosphere I feel at home in. To me acting is more than a job, or having a star part; it's a way of life, and I still get the same feeling of excitement when I get a call to go to the studio. I never know where it may lead.

Chapter 8
The Work Scene

Introduction

The theatre, say those who work in it, is in a bad way. There are fewer formal theatres open than there used to be, both in London and the regions, and the increasing cost of seat prices, fares and eating out has made an evening at the theatre an expensive pleasure. The West End, where it costs £100,000 to stage even a modest production and needs at least three months of full houses to begin to break even, has been hard hit, with theatres going dark and up for sale. It is not, on the face of it, a good moment to be starting out in the theatre.

But the picture is not all gloomy. New theatres have been built with public money: in London, on the South Bank and in the Barbican, while a number of regional repertory companies have new homes more suited in size to local audiences than the palaces of the Victorian and Edwardian eras. New, too, has been the steady increase in small companies performing in a variety of venues from clubs and pubs to church halls, community centres, libraries and parks. Many are ephemeral, some perhaps of doubtful worth, but they are evidence that the theatre is alive and well and powered by energy and enthusiasm.

The ideal progress for a young actor is to start in a regional rep, get some experience of television and films, and then join a major company or break into the commercial theatre. This was the experience of Ian Charleson, who trained at LAMDA where he was spotted by Frank Dunlop, who took him into the Young Vic company. He made his professional debut at the Edinburgh Festival, and went on to work with the Cambridge Theatre Company, the National Theatre, and the RSC at Stratford and in London. But it was his part as the Flying Scotsman Eric Liddell, in the film *Chariots of Fire*, that put him on the map. As he said in an interview:

> Since *Chariots* I've been taken seriously as an actor and a leading man. I'd been young and up-and-coming for years but nobody ever put their money where their mouth is and gave me a real corker where I had to carry the whole piece . . .

He was talking about his part as the cool gambler Sky Masterson in the NT's production of *Guys and Dolls*, a role that convinced him that at last he had arrived.

Roughly speaking the theatre scene is divided between London and the regions, with a certain amount of overlap.

London

The Commercial Theatre

The label 'commercial' refers not only to the aim of making a profit — the aim too of most subsidised theatres — but to the way in which any profits are distributed to the production's backers instead of being ploughed back into some form of charitable trust.

The need to make a profit tends to influence commercial managements to play safe by putting on musicals, thrillers and light comedies, for which there is an assured audience including a high proportion of tourists. More adventurous new plays are often launched at subsidised non-central theatres in residential areas of London, such as the Greenwich Theatre and the Hampstead Theatre, with managements taking an option to transfer them to the West End if they look like being a success.

West End plays are often chosen as a vehicle for star names, and sometimes tried out first in the touring theatres of the provinces, but this practice seems to be dying out in favour of preview performances with reduced ticket prices.

Only actors with full Equity membership are eligible to work in the West End.

Subsidised Theatres

It may seem inaccurate to consider the Royal Shakespeare Company a London company, since it was founded at Stratford-upon-Avon (where it is still a major attraction and has two theatres, the Memorial Theatre, and The Other Place, a small studio theatre for experimental productions and new plays). But since 1960, when Peter — now Sir Peter — Hall first brought the company to the Aldwych, the RSC has been an important part of the London theatre scene, offering a challenge to the National Theatre on the South Bank. In 1982, the RSC moved into the Barbican Theatre, which has been specially designed as its London home and where there is also a studio space, The Pit, to house transfers from The Other Place.

The company now has four theatres, makes an annual visit to the North, has occasional transfers to the West End, and goes on international tours, which allows it to offer its actors some degree of security. Players are initially hired for 60 weeks, to cover two seasons. Salaries do not compare with those in the commercial theatre — the actors' minimum is around £110 a week — but there is also the lure of television and films.

The National Theatre also offers actors the experience of being part of a company — the trend has been increasingly towards the Brechtian ideal of a company playing with an anti-heroic, non-star bias — and the greater security of longterm contracts. Actors tend in the first instance to be hired for a single play, which may stay in the repertoire for two or three years, and it is up to the director whether they are offered parts in other plays.

The NT is in effect several companies putting on plays at its three theatres: the proscenium-stage Lyttleton, the arena-stage Olivier, and the small rectangular Cottesloe, with a simple floor space and galleries on three sides.

Appearing with the NT is not particularly lucrative — minimum salaries are around £110 a week.

Both companies have benefited from the work of another subsidised theatre, the Royal Court, which was taken over by the English Stage Company in 1956. It has been called 'a writers' theatre', since it set out to find and encourage new playwrights. John Osborne, John Arden, Arnold Wesker, Edward Bond and David Storey are among its successes, and the ESC also brought to London the work of foreign dramatists such as Bertolt Brecht, Samuel Beckett, Max Frisch and Jean Genet.

The Royal Court pioneered plays that reflected and were critical of contemporary life — many of its writers were committed socialists — and it brought into the theatre voices and attitudes that had not been heard before. Its influence was felt throughout the theatre and in the cinema, and many of its writers have since become 'respectable' enough for the national companies and the commercial theatre.

Less obviously influential but an interesting experiment is Sir Bernard Miles's Mermaid Theatre, which opened with the aim of bridging the gap between highbrow and lowbrow and has presented a mixture of neglected classics, musicals, new plays, and translations of foreign plays.

London, too, has its fringe theatre, an assortment of theatre clubs, lunchtime theatre and pub theatre, such as the Gate at the Latchmere and the Kings Head theatre club at Islington. They tend to be small areas with seating for fewer than 100, in which productions can be staged with the minimum of costumes and props. Typical is the Orange Tree at Richmond, an upstairs room in a pub that provides an informal setting for new and experimental plays, which encourages the audience to concentrate on the ideas and words. American plays and hits from the Edinburgh Festival fringe are the speciality of the Gate theatres in Notting Hill Gate and Battersea.

The Regions

Repertory Companies

These are the companies in which young actors tend to make their debuts, and according to the latest edition of *Spotlight* there are more than 70 of them.

The actors perform in a variety of buildings, from ornate Victorian touring theatres to the many civic theatres built during the 1960s and early 70s, and their artistic policies are equally diverse. The Yvonne Arnaud at Guildford, for example, doesn't have a permanent company and uses actors from London — one or two faces made familiar by television are a popular draw — to stage thrillers, comedies and safe revivals of plays likely to appeal to a middle-aged, conservative audience. The Victoria Theatre, Stoke-on-Trent, set up by Stephen Joseph, a pioneer of theatre-in-the-round and the discoverer of Alan Ayckbourn, has had a policy of encouraging new writers and devising plays based on local history. Many other local theatres have been similarly adventurous.

The new theatres have been designed to include restaurants and coffee bars and often have spacious foyers suitable for exhibitions, and this has helped to encourage the idea of the theatre as a focus for local cultural activity, open also during the day. They have been financed by grants from the Arts Council, the local authorities — municipal pride has often been more important than an actual interest in the theatre — and money raised by public appeals, and depend heavily on continuing subsidies. This has its effect on the programme, with poor returns leading to calls from the board of directors, who usually include representatives of the local authority, for more popular fare, though some reps have managed to build up audiences with adventurous taste.

Gone are the days when repertory companies performed twice nightly and actors were expected to give 12 performances a week *and* rehearse next week's play — and all for less than £10 a week. Nowadays plays run for at least two weeks, often longer, and some companies run plays in repertory. Minimum Equity rates for performers start at around £80 a week.

Alternative and Community Theatre

Almost anything goes in this area, which has as one of its most important aims attracting audiences who don't normally go to the theatre. Many of the performances don't take place in theatres anyway, but in venues like church halls, clubs, pubs, community centres and parks, that are more accessible, especially to a working-class audience.

Most companies are small — perhaps half a dozen actors and a director, maybe friends who joined up at drama school or college — and they usually need the minimum in stage equipment and can put on a show anywhere. Some receive subsidies from regional arts associations or local authorities; others are run on a shoestring and live in hope that some kind of backing will be forthcoming. Working as a cooperative is popular, and this is not the kind of theatre for anyone who aims to make money: the rewards are strictly in terms of job satisfaction.

Although some companies aim just to entertain, many have some kind of message or social purpose. One such is Combination, a group in the East End of London, who aim to be 'epic, out-front, popular, committed, multi-cultural and rooted in the experience of a working-class community'. Feminism is a popular cause, with groups like Bloomers (a three-woman comedy team), Scarlet Harlets, and Monstrous Regiment. In contrast, the Platform 6 Theatre Company is 'a male company examining male stereotypes and power and its causes', and aims 'to provide anti-sexist, anti-racist theatre for schools and the community'.

Community theatre, as its name suggests, seeks to work closely with local people, running workshops and devising dramatic happenings dealing with local issues and topical matters such as town-planning, unemployment, and the threat of nuclear missiles. This is the theatre of those who see drama as a force for social change and want to reach new audiences. Such groups are often united by a cause other than acting, and may disband after a couple of years.

Many alternative theatre companies are concerned with a particular theme. Cliffhanger, for example, goes in for original comedy inspired by pulp literature, B-movies, soap operas and correspondence columns; Green Fields & Far Away devotes itself to Irish and Irish-related drama; the Mikron Theatre Company tours canals and riverside pubs with shows about the history of the inland waterways and the people who have helped restore them.

Many companies are known only locally — and indeed bringing theatre to some of the more remote areas is often one of their aims — but some catch the eye of the national press from time to time. It's an area for experiments and informality, in which originality and ingenuity thrive and limited resources force performers and audiences to rethink the purpose and potential of theatre.

The *British Alternative Theatre Directory* has a useful list of alternative, fringe and community theatre companies, with brief details of their policies and personnel.

Children's Theatre

This ranges from the long-established Unicorn Theatre, which puts on five main productions for the under 12s and three studio shows for infants as well as a touring show; and the Whirligig, which commissions full-length musicals with enticing titles like *The Potters of Cabbage Patch Corner*; to tiny companies performing in a variety of venues. Some, like the All Day Suckers, are avowedly working-class; some, like Fairplay (which describes itself as 'a catalyst for social change'), have a definite aim; others like Cuckoo are specifically for the under-fives, while yet others are for the 7-11 age group.

Programmes demand a mixture of skills, from mime and clowning to manipulating puppets and Punch and Judy, and usually involve some degree of audience participation through singing and playing games. Some take the form of workshops that encourage the children themselves to perform.

This is an area most likely to appeal to those who have studied drama from the educational point of view.

Theatre-in-Education

A number of repertory theatres have theatre-in-education companies attached to them, and there are also young people's theatre companies aimed at encouraging young people themselves to perform.

The companies take productions to school children, putting on performances that may relate directly to their studies, such as the current GCE set plays, as well as dramatisations of topical social, economic and political problems. One company, for example, has devised programmes about working on a North Sea oil rig and the issue of working mothers.

Some companies have no regular base but tour schools within an area, taking all their equipment in a van. Such shoestring operations may last a couple of years before the members go their separate ways, often into teaching.

Chapter 9
Obligations

Equity

The British Actors Equity Association was formed in 1930 and became an official trade union ten years later. Its members cover all aspects of the entertainments industry, from actors, directors and designers to dancers, singers, stage managers, stunt performers, ice skaters and variety artists, and they are all eligible for election to the managing Council of 65 members who are elected every two years by a postal ballot of the entire membership.

The aim of Equity is to protect the interests of its members by ensuring that they are not exploited and receive a fair return for their work, and it does this by insisting on the use of standard contracts that specify minimum fees and regulate conditions of employment such as hours of work and redundancy payments.

The use of such contracts could not be enforced unless Equity was in a position to insist on a closed shop, and so Equity members are forbidden to work with non-members, and there are very few companies that operate outside Equity rules.

In a profession with a spectacularly high rate of unemployment — some three-quarters of Equity members are likely to be unemployed at any one time — it makes sense to try and control the number of new recruits each year and to restrict their immediate right to some of the plums. Thus casting agreements between the employers and Equity debar newcomers from being considered for work in a number of fields. These include the West End theatre, the major subsidised companies, major pantomimes and tours, feature films, television and radio, and TV commercials. Exceptions are occasionally made to this — the young actor who played the lead in *Another Country*, a play about a boys' school, is an example — but the matter has to be considered by a joint Council of representatives from management and Equity, and management have to make out a strong case for insisting that no existing member of Equity would be suitable for the part. (In the example given, the young actor was allowed to appear.)

Activities

Some idea of the scope of Equity's work can be gained from the 1981-2 Annual Report, which summarised its activities as follows:

> Equity, with a staff of just over 50 (little larger than it was 15 years ago), now negotiates each year 24 major industrial agreements and a far larger number of local or company agreements. Nearly 40 permanent committees of members hold a total of around 400 meetings a year. About one million pounds is collected and accounted for in fees and subscriptions and 25,000 reminder notices are sent out to members. The total amount of money received by members as a result of claims and recoveries dealt with by Equity and residual payments for television films, videogramme sales and gramophone royalties on sales of original cast recordings, amounts to nearly half a million pounds. Members change their addresses at the staggering rate of 200 per week, and all these changes are recorded by the staff. Our switchboard deals with some 76,000 telephone calls a year.

Among topics discussed during the year were the Sunday opening of theatres (members are to vote on this), the employment of performers from outside the UK, the campaign against theatre cuts and VAT, minimum salaries, a pension scheme for dancers, Channel Four, cable and satellite television, and the piracy of sound and video recordings. Such matters underline the need for a strong and well-organised union to protect the rights of individual performers.

Getting an Equity Card

Membership of Equity is therefore a necessary first step for anyone who wants to appear in the professional theatre, but getting an Equity card sounds rather like Catch 22: you can't appear in the theatre until you've got a card, but you can't get one until you've been offered an Equity-approved contract.

So how is the newcomer expected to make a start? Well, every year reps, theatre-in-education companies, children's theatre companies and some fringe organisations are allowed to take on a limited number of newcomers under a quota system that has been agreed between the employers and Equity. The usual allowance is two actors per company and one assistant stage manager per team, and it has recently been decided to reserve half the number of cards issued for graduates of accredited courses.

The lucky newcomers are granted provisional membership and become entitled to full membership after working for 40 weeks in approved work. The 40 weeks don't have to be consecutive, but can be totted up over a number of jobs. Newcomers are also allowed to appear as chorus singers and dancers in provincial productions not classified as 'number one' seasons or tours, as ASMs with no obligation to act or understudy, in the summer seasons or tours of provincial productions, or as singers, dancers, directors, assistant directors or designers with any company offering a standard Equity contract. Such jobs all count towards full membership, but work as an extra or walk-on in television, films, or commercials, isn't usually accepted as a qualification for membership.

Subscriptions

Members pay an entrance fee of £15 and then an annual subscription based on their income. In 1982 the rates were £32 for up to £5,000, £52 for £5,001 to £7,000, £72 for £7,001 to £10,000 and so on up to a maximum contribution, with a reduced subscription of £20 for those earning less than £3,000 a year.

Once a full member, you retain your membership as long as you continue to pay your subscription. Members who want to leave the profession for some years can apply to have their membership suspended.

Subscriptions are paid direct to Equity or collected by the Equity deputy, who is usually elected by the other members of the company and undertakes to maintain contact between members and Equity and help sort out any complaints or disputes with the management.

Services

Equity estimates that the majority of their members pay 38½p per week for services that range far beyond contracts and theatre conditions. They include:

Free legal advice on any dispute about professional engagements from the Equity legal officer and, if necessary, Equity's solicitors.

Legal aid and protection that could result in the recovery of money.

Advice on National Insurance problems and procedure. In some cases members can be represented at appeals and tribunals.

General advice on income tax and VAT.

The distribution of royalty payments (for records and re-runs of TV film series) which are made en bloc to Equity and then passed on to the member concerned.

A copy of the monthly *Equity Journal*.

Insurance advice (see below).

Small grants and loans from the benevolent fund to help members in emergencies.

Special discounts on a variety of goods offered by a list of shops.

Insurance

Equity members of one or more years' standing can take advantage of two insurance schemes that have been specially

tailored to suit the hazards of the profession and of backstage life. The Accident Benefit offers 24-hour cover for
most types of accidents, and the Backstage Cover insures
against loss or damage to personal property from any
backstage cause.

British Actors' Equity Advisory Insurance Service Ltd,
131 New London Road, Chelmsford, Essex CM2 0QZ
(0245 51581) are insurance brokers who specialise in giving
Equity members advice about insurance, mortgages and
pension schemes, and enable them to obtain normal cover
at standard and sometimes discount rates. It's well worth
asking them about motor insurance and cover for any
personal assets, such as your best feature, be it beautiful
teeth or marvellous legs. An injury could well mean an
alarming drop in your income. Pensions may seem a long
way off to those just starting out, but pension premiums
are one way of saving and there are generous tax benefits
on even the smallest premiums.

National Insurance

National insurance contributions are compulsory and
entitle you to:

   unemployment benefit
   sickness and invalidity benefit
   maternity allowance
   widow's pension
   guardian allowance
   child's special allowance
   retirement pension
   death grant.

You are liable for Class 1 contributions when working on
any job that brings in more than a minimum sum (in 1982
the lower earnings limit was £29.50 a week), and your
contributions are calculated as a percentage of your earnings
up to a maximum amount (in 1982 the upper earnings
limit was £220 a week) and deducted by your employer.

Income Tax

Although the majority of Equity members pay Class 1 National Insurance contributions as employees, for tax purposes they are usually treated as self-employed and taxed under a system known as Schedule D. This involves them in calculating their income at the end of the fiscal year (which runs from April to April), submitting an account of their earnings and expenses, and then paying the tax due in two instalments on 1 January and 1 July (interest is charged on any tax overdue).

From time to time actors appear in the bankruptcy court with horrendous tax debts which have accumulated because of the uncertain and uneven level of their income (vast one moment, non-existent the next) and because Schedule D tax is always paid in arrears, so that the tax on a good year may have to be paid in a year when earnings have shrunk to less than half. So don't deceive yourself if you do happen to have a particularly good year — about a third properly belongs to the Inland Revenue.

Although you can wrestle with the tax authorities yourself, even if you have only a modest income it's usually worth having your tax return done by an accountant. Of course you will have to pay, but the fees are an allowable expense and the advice should save you more than enough to cover them and spare a lot of hassle.

Some accountants specialise in theatrical clients and have the advantage of knowing all the ins and outs of allowable expenses. Ask around among theatrical friends or follow up the advertisements in the *Equity Journal* and *The Stage*.

Allowable Expenses

One advantage of being taxed under Schedule D is that it does recognise professional expenses. These are things you have to pay for in the course of earning your living, and it may be helpful to know the sort of expenses that are likely to be accepted as necessary. They include:

make-up
hairdressing
chiropody (mainly dancers)
theatre laundry
Equity subscription
tips to dressers, call-boys, stage door-keepers etc
the cleaning, repair and replacement of wardrobe and
    props (usually an expense allowable to variety artists)
agent's fees
singing and dancing lessons
taxis on tour
telephone calls and postage (on letters applying for jobs
    and fan mail)
publicity photographs
advertisement in *Spotlight*
any magazines or newspapers (such as *Radio Times*, *The
    Stage*) bought to keep up to date
any books, scripts etc needed for the study of a part
likewise tapes or records
travelling expenses to auditions etc
accommodation expenses while on tour
accountant's fees.

You should keep a careful note of all such expenses and
keep the bills too, in case you are asked for proof of your
claims.

Although the theatre may sound an improvident way of
life, insurance, tax, VAT (only payable on higher-bracket
incomes), and pensions are areas that require prudent
management, and the image of the carefree actor, drifting
through life on an unworldly course, is misleading. Modern
life, alas, is full of obligations that catch up with you
sooner or later, and learning to manage money — especially
when you haven't much — is very important.

Part 2
Chapter 10
Useful Addresses

Chapter 2

Daily conducted tours of the National Theatre begin at
10.15 am, 12.30 pm, 12.45 pm, 5.30 pm and 6.00 pm,
except on Wednesdays and Saturdays when there are no
12.30 pm or 5.30 pm tours. Each tour lasts about 1¼ hours,
and is limited to 30 people. Bookings are accepted at least
4 weeks in advance: by post or at the Lyttelton Information
Desk between 10.00 am and 11.00 pm. For further information, ring 01-633 0880.

Chapter 3

Stage Schools Offering Full-Time Education

Bush Davies Schools Ltd, Charters Towers, East Grinstead, Sussex
Italia Conti Academy of Theatre Arts Ltd, Avondale Hall, Landor
  Road, London SW9 9PH
Corona Stage Schools, 26 Wellesley Road, London W4
Elliott-Clarke School, 63 Rodney Street, Liverpool 1
Redroofs Theatre School, Littlewick Green, Maidenhead, Berkshire
Barbara Speake Stage School, East Acton Lane, London W3
Tring Park (Arts Educational), Tring, Hertfordshire
Sylvia Young Theatre School, 44 Drury Lane, London WC2

For stage schools offering part-time training see the current
British Theatre Directory and *Contacts*.

Young People's Theatre Companies

These are just some of the companies that give young

people a chance to take part in workshops and productions.

Yvonne Arnaud Theatre, Millbrook, Guildford, Surrey GU1 3UX
Barnstormers Youth Theatre Group, 107 Ladies Mile Road,
    Patcham, Brighton
Common Stock Theatre Company, 182 Hammersmith Road,
    London W6
Contact Theatre Community Drama Project, The Brickhouse,
    Devas Street, Manchester M15 6JA
Croydon Young People's Theatre, c/o Ashcroft Theatre,
    Fairfield Halls, Park Lane, Croydon
Gorton Workshop, 18 Hawthorn Grove, Heaton Moor, Stockport,
    Cheshire
Greenwich Young People's Theatre, Burrage Road, London SE18
Langley Theatre Group, Adult Education Centre, Wood Street,
    Middleton, Manchester
Manchester Youth Theatre, 57 Hulme Hall Road, Cheadle Hulme,
    Stockport SK8 6JX
Merseyside Young People's Theatre Company, 5 Hope Street,
    Liverpool
Royal Court Young People's Theatre Scheme, Royal Court Theatre,
    Sloane Square, London SW1
Anna Scher Children's Theatre, 70 Barnsbury Road, London N1
Scottish Youth Theatre, 48 Albany Street, Edinburgh
Sideshow Young People's Theatre, contact Shaun McKenna,
    52 Woodcut Sandling Lane, Maidstone, Kent
Young National Trust Theatre, National Trust, 42 Queen Anne's
    Gate, London SW1
Young Vic, 66 The Cut, London SE1.

Theatre-in-education companies tend to be more involved
in putting on shows for young people, but some also invite
audience participation.

Regional Repertory Theatres with Theatre-in-Education Companies

These include: Octagon, Bolton; Mercury, Colchester;
Belgrade, Coventry; Playhouse, Derby; Redgrave, Farnham;
Citizens, Glasgow; Harrogate Theatre; Wolsey, Ipswich;
Duke's Playhouse, Lancaster; Thorndike, Leatherhead;
Playhouse, Leeds; Playhouse, Nottingham; Theatre Royal,
Plymouth; Crucible, Sheffield; Palace, Watford; Palace,
Westcliff; Theatre Royal, York.

Organisations

National Council of Theatre for Young People, 9 Fitzroy Square,
    London W1
National Youth Theatre of Great Britain, Shaw Theatre,
    100 Euston Road, London NW1 2AJ
Standing Conference of Young People's Theatre, c/o Bruvvers,
    24 Shields Road, Byker, Newcastle-upon-Tyne.

Chapter 4

Conference of Drama Schools, c/o The Rose Bruford College,
    Lamorbey Park, Sidcup, Kent
National Council for Drama Training, 5 Tavistock Place,
    London WC1

Drama Schools with Accredited Acting Courses

Arts Educational School, Golden Lane House, Golden Lane,
    London EC1Y 0RR
Birmingham School of Speech Training and Dramatic Art,
    45 Church Road, Edgbaston, Birmingham B15 3SW
Bristol Old Vic School, 1-2 Downside Road, Clifton,
    Bristol BS8 2XF
Central School of Speech and Drama, Embassy Theatre,
    Eton Avenue, London NW3 3HY
Drama Centre, London, 176 Prince of Wales Road, London NW5
Guildford School of Acting and Drama, 20 Buryfields, Guildford,
    Surrey GU2 5AZ
Guildhall School of Music and Drama, Barbican, London EC2Y 8DT
London Academy of Music and Dramatic Art (LAMDA), Tower
    House, 226 Cromwell Road, London SW5 0SR
Manchester Polytechnic, School of Theatre, Department of
    Communication Arts and Design, Capitol Building, School Lane,
    Didsbury, Manchester M20 1OHT
Rose Bruford College of Speech and Drama, Lamorbey Park,
    Sidcup, Kent DA15 9DF
Royal Academy of Dramatic Art (RADA), 62-64 Gower Street,
    London WC1E 6ED
Royal Scottish Academy of Music and Drama, St George's Place,
    Glasgow G2 1BS
Webber Douglas Academy of Dramatic Art, 30-36 Clareville Street,
    London SW7 5AP
Welsh College of Music and Drama, Castle Grounds, Cathays Park,
    Cardiff CF1 3ER

Other Members of the Conference of Drama Schools

East 15 Acting School, Hatfields, Rectory Lane, Loughton, Essex
Mountview Theatre School, 104 Crouch Hill, London N8
Queen Margaret College School of Drama, 36 Clerwood Terrace,
    Edinburgh EH12 8TS.

Grants

Arts Council awards: details from the Drama Director, the Arts
    Council, 105 Piccadilly, London W1.
Grant booklets available direct from: Department of Education and
    Science, Information Division, Elizabeth House, York Road,
    London SE1; the Scottish Education Department, St Andrew's
    House, Edinburgh; the Department of Education for Northern
    Ireland, Rathgael House, Balloo Road, Bangor.

Theatre Design Courses

Central School of Art and Design, Southampton Row, London WC1
City of Birmingham Polytechnic, School of Theatre Design, Gosta
    Green, Birmingham B4 7ET
Croydon College, School of Art and Design, Fairfield, Croydon
Slade School of Art, Gower Street, London WC1
Theatre Design Course, Camperdown House, Half Moon Passage,
    London E1
Trent Polytechnic, Dryden Street, Nottingham NC1 4BU
Wimbledon School of Art, Merton Hall Road, Wimbledon SW19
    3QA
West Sussex College of Design, Union Place, Worthing, West Sussex.

Theatre Wardrobe Courses

Canterbury College of Art, New Dover Road, Canterbury, Kent
London College of Fashion, 20 John Prince's Street, London W1
Mabel Fletcher Technical College, Sandown Road, Liverpool L15
    4JB.

Technical Courses

Association of British Theatre Technicians, 4-7 Great Pulteney
    Street, London W1
Croydon College, Fairfield, Croydon CR9 1DX
Hammersmith and West London College, Airlie Gardens, London
    W8
Paddington College, Paddington Green, London W2 1NB.

Directors' Training

Arts Council, 105 Piccadilly, London W1V 0AU
The Drama Studio, Grange Court, 1 Grange Road, London W5 5QN
Regional Theatre Trainee Director Scheme, No 1 Marine Parade,
    Bognor Regis, West Sussex PO21 2LT.

Chapter 5

Universities' Central Council on Admissions, PO Box 28,
    Cheltenham, Gloucestershire GL50 1HY.

University Courses

University of Birmingham, Drama and Theatre Arts Department,
    PO Box 363, Birmingham B15 2TT
University of Bristol, Drama Department, 29 Park Row, Bristol BS1
    5LT
University of Exeter, School of English, Drama Department,
    Thornlea, New North Road, Exeter EX4 4JZ
University of Glasgow, Department of Drama, 17 Lilybank Gardens,
    Glasgow G12
University of Hull, Drama Department, Gulbenkian Centre, The
    University, Hull, North Humberside HU6 7RX
University of Kent at Canterbury, Board of Studies in Drama,
    UKC, Canterbury, Kent
University of Lancaster, Department of Theatre Studies, Nuffield
    Theatre, The University, Bailrigg, Lancaster LA1 4YW
University of London, Goldsmiths' College, Drama Department,
    Lewisham Way, New Cross, London SE14 6NW
University of London, Royal Holloway College, Department of
    Drama and Theatre Studies, Egham Hill, Egham, Surrey
University of London, Westfield College, Kidderpore Avenue,
    London NW3 7ST
University of Loughborough, Technology, English and Drama
    Department, Ashby Road, Loughborough, Leicestershire
    LE11 3TU
Victoria University of Manchester, Drama Department, Oxford
    Road, Manchester M13 9PL
University of Surrey, General Studies Department, Guildford,
    Surrey
University of Wales, University College of Wales, Aberystwyth,
    Department of Drama, 1 Laura Place, Aberystwyth, Dyfed
    SY23 2AU
University of Wales, University College of North Wales, Bangor,
    Department of Drama, Bangor, Gwynedd LL57 2DG
University of Warwick, Department of Theatre Studies, Coventry
    CV4 7AL.

CNAA Courses

Bulmershe College of Higher Education, Division of Drama,
Woodlands Avenue, Earley, Reading RG6 1HY
Crewe and Alsager College, Faculty of Arts, Alsager, Staffordshire
Dartington College of Arts, Department of Theatre, Totnes, Devon
Huddersfield Polytechnic, Department of English Studies, Drama
Section, Queensgate, Huddersfield HD1 3DH
Leicester Polytechnic, Drama Department, Scraptoft Campus,
Scraptoft, Leicester
Middlesex Polytechnic, Enquiry Office, 114 Chase Side, London
N14 5PN
Newcastle Upon Tyne Polytechnic, School of Creative and
Performing Arts, Lipman Building, Sandyford Road,
Newcastle-upon-Tyne NE1 8ST
Trent Polytechnic, Creative Arts Department, Clifton Main Site,
Clifton, Nottingham
Polytechnic of Wales, Arts and Languages Department,
Buttrills Road, Barry, South Glamorgan
King Alfred's College, Sparkford Road, Winchester SO22 4NR.

CNAA *Directory of Courses* available from Council for National
Academic Awards, 344-354 Gray's Inn Road, London WC1
BTI and DATEC *Directory* available from the British Theatre
Institute, 30 Clareville Street, London SW7.

Colleges of Higher Education Courses

Bretton Hall College, School of Drama and Theatre Studies, West
Bretton, Wakefield, West Yorks
Chester College of Higher Education, Department of Drama,
Cheyney Road, Chester CH1 4BJ
Ilkley College, Department of Performing and Visual Arts, Wells
Road, Ilkley LS29 9RD
City of Liverpool College of Higher Education, Department of
Drama, Prescot, Merseyside L34 1NP
Nene College, School of Humanities, Moulton Park Campus,
Boughton Green Road, Northampton NN2 7AL
Nonington College, Nonington, Dover, Kent CT15 4HH
North Cheshire College, Department of Theatre Studies, Padgate
Campus, Fearnhead, Warrington WA2 0DB
College of Ripon and York St John, Department of Dance, Drama,
Movement, Film and Television, Lord Mayor's Walk, York
YO3 7EX
Roehampton Institute of Higher Education, Roehampton Lane,
London SW15
Rolle College, Department of Theatre Arts, Exmouth, Devon EX8
2AT

Trinity and All Saints' College, Drama Department, Brownberrie
   Lane, Horsforth, Leeds LS18 5HD.

Chapter 6

City University, Arts Administration Studies, The Centre for Arts,
   Northampton Square, London EC1V 0HB.

Professional Casting Report, 280 Lordship Lane, London SE22

The Spotlight Casting Directory, 42-43 Cranbourn Street, London
   WC2H 7AP

The Stage and Television Today, 47 Bermondsey Street, London
   SE1 3XT.

Chapter 7

Cordon Bleu Cookery School (London) Ltd, 114 Marylebone Lane,
   London W1

Message Minders, Orient House, 42-45 New Broad Street, London
   EC2M 1QY

For details of Pitman's shorthand courses: Pitman's Central College,
   154 Southampton Row, London WC1B 5AX

Notes on Radio Drama is available from the Script Editor, Drama
   (Radio) BBC, Broadcasting House, London W1A 1AA

For details of Speedwriting courses: Speedwriting International
   Centre, 59-61 South Molton Street, London W1Y 2AX

Time Out, Tower House, Southampton Street, London WC2

Writers' & Artists' Yearbook, published by A. & C. Black,
   35 Bedford Row, London WC1R 4JH.

Chapter 9

British Actors' Equity Advisory Insurance Service Ltd, 131 New
   London Road, Chelmsford, Essex CM2 0QZ

British Actors' Equity Association, 8 Harley Street, London W1N 2AB
   Northern office: 85 Mosley Street, Manchester M2 3LG
   Scottish office: 65 Bath Street, Glasgow G2 2BX
   Welsh office: 34 Queen Street, Cardiff CF1 4BW.

Chapter 11
Reading List

Reference

British Alternative Theatre Directory, edited by Catherine Itzin. John Offord Publications. Published annually. A guide to smallscale companies, children's theatre and young people's theatre, with a directory of playwrights, directors and designers.

British Theatre Directory. John Offord Publications in association with the British Theatre Institute. Published annually. Lists theatres (with size, seating, technical details), municipal entertainment, theatre companies, festivals, agents, publishers, training and education, TV and radio companies, theatre critics, etc.

British Theatre Institute and DATEC Directory of Drama Courses in Higher Education. Published annually by the BTI. Covers courses in drama schools, universities, polytechnics, colleges of higher education, and colleges of art.

Contacts. Published annually in May by *The Spotlight*. See page 109.

Practical

Drama and Dance. Choice of Careers booklet no 98, produced by the Manpower Services Commission

Going on the Stage. The report of the Committee of Inquiry set up by the Calouste Gulbenkian Foundation into professional training for drama. 1975

Clive Barker, *Theatre Games*. Methuen. 1977. A new approach to drama training

Peter Barkworth, *About Acting*. Secker & Warburg. 1980. Advice from a distinguished actor based on his experience of teaching at RADA

Michael Billington, *The Modern Actor*. Hamish Hamilton. 1973

Ronald Hayman, *How to Read a Play*. Methuen. 1977

John Hodgson (editor), *The Uses of Drama*. Methuen. 1972. An anthology of pieces about acting as a social and educational force

John Hodgson and Ernest Richards, *Improvisation*. Methuen. 1968

Keith Johnstone, *Impro*. Methuen. 2nd edition 1981. Improvisation and the theatre

John Pick, *Arts Administration*. E. & F. N. Spon

Richard Pilbrow, *Stage Lighting*. Cassell. Revised edition 1979

Constantin Stanislavski, *An Actor Prepares, Building a Character, Creating a Role, My Life in Art*. Methuen

Clive Swift, *The Job of Acting*. Harrap. 1976. A racy practical guide to working in the theatre, with advice on everything from voice-overs and money-earning tasks to marriage

Clive Swift, *The Performing World of the Actor*. Hamish Hamilton. 1981.

Background

Sally Beauman, *The Royal Shakespeare Company: A History of Ten Decades*. Oxford. 1982

John Russell Brown, *A Short Guide to Modern British Drama*. Heinemann Educational

John Elsom, *Theatre Outside London*. Macmillan. 1971. A survey of the post-war repertory movement that also considers the theatre's role in the community and as a social force

Brian Forbes, *That Despicable Race*. Elm Tree. 1980. A history of the British acting tradition

Howard Goorney, *The Theatre Workshop Story*. Methuen. 1981

Ronald Hayman, *The Set-Up*. Methuen. 1973. A stimulating survey of the English theatre today that explains how theatres are run, the organisation of big companies, reps, fringe, the role of the Arts Council etc

Jim Hiley, *Theatre At Work*. Routledge & Kegan Paul. 1981. The story of the National Theatre's production of Brecht's *Galileo*

Macmillan Modern Dramatists series, *Contemporary American Dramatists, American Alternative Theatre, Georg Buchner, Georges Feydeau and Eugene Labiche, Harold Pinter*. Includes biographical details, survey of development, analysis of best-known plays, bibliography, photographs

Leon Rubin, *The Nicholas Nickleby Story*. Heinemann. 1981. The story of the highly successful Royal Shakespeare Company production

David Selbourne, *The Making of A Midsummer Night's Dream*. Methuen. 1982. An eye-witness account of Peter Brook's 1970 production from the first rehearsal to the first night

John Russell Taylor, *Anger and After*. Methuen. 3rd edition 1977. A guide to British drama post John Osborne

John Russell Taylor, *The Second Wave*. Methuen. 2nd edition 1978. British drama of the 1960s

Simon Trussler (editor), *New Theatre Voices of the 70s*. Methuen.
    1981. Interviews from *Theatre Quarterly* 1970-80
Irving Wardle, *The Theatres of George Devine*. Methuen. 1979.

Actors

Dirk Bogarde, *A Postillion Struck by Lightning*. Chatto & Windus.
    1977. *Snakes and Ladders*. Chatto & Windus. 1978
John Gielgud, *An Actor and His Time*. Sidgwick & Jackson. 1979
Ronald Hayman, *John Gielgud*. Heinemann. 1971
Garry O'Connor, *Ralph Richardson. An Actor's Life*. Hodder. 1982
Laurence Olivier, *Confessions of an Actor*. Weidenfeld & Nicolson.
    1982
Donald Sinden, *A Touch of the Memoirs*. Hodder. 1982
Peter Ustinov, *Dear Me*. Heinemann. 1977.

Plays

Faber and Faber publish a number of playwrights including
    Samuel Beckett, Alan Bennett, T. S. Eliot, Jean Genet,
    Christopher Hampton, David Hare, Peter Nichols, John Osborne,
    Tom Stoppard.
Methuen publish plays and screenplays by John Arden, Brendan
    Behan, Edward Bond, Bertolt Brecht, Noel Coward, Joe Orton,
    Harold Pinter, Stephen Poliakoff and other classic and modern
    playwrights.
Methuen Student Editions: plays by John Arden, Bertolt Brecht,
    Shelagh Delany, Harold Pinter, and Oscar Wilde that have
    become modern classics. Include chronology of playwright's
    life and work, background introduction, discussion of various
    interpretations, photographs from stage and film productions.
Methuen Young Drama: new plays for young audiences from youth
    theatre groups and theatre-in-education companies. Also plays
    from the Thames Television Theatre Box series.
Best Radio Plays of 1978, 1979, 1980, 1981, 1982. Methuen.
    Winners of the Giles Cooper Awards sponsored by Methuen and
    the BBC.
William Shakespeare: the RSC use the New Penguin edition
    (Penguin Books) which has an introduction, commentary and
    reading list. The Arden Shakespeare (Methuen) is a scholarly
    edition with a long introduction and detailed notes. Both
    editions issue the plays in single volumes and as paperbacks.